Microsoft® Office
Access™ 2007 Plain & Simple

Curtis Frye

PUBLISHED BY
Microsoft Press
A Division of Microsoft Corporation
One Microsoft Way
Redmond, Washington 98052-6399

Library of Congress Control Number: 2006937713

Printed and bound in the United States of America.

1 2 3 4 5 6 7 8 9   QWT   2 1 0 9 8 7

Distributed in Canada by H.B. Fenn and Company Ltd.

A CIP catalogue record for this book is available from the British Library.

Microsoft Press books are available through booksellers and distributors worldwide. For further information about international editions, contact your local Microsoft Corporation office or contact Microsoft Press International directly at fax (425) 936-7329. Visit our Web site at www.microsoft.com/mspress. Send comments to mspinput@microsoft.com.

Acquisitions Editor: Juliana Aldous Atkinson
Project Editor: Kathleen Atkins
Project Manager: Joell Smith-Borne of Abshier House
Compositor: Debbie Berman of Abshier House
Indexer: Kelly Dobbs Henthorne of Abshier House

Body Part No. X12-65202

To Virginia.

Contents

1 Introduction: About This Book 1

2 What's New in Access 2007 5

3 Introducing Access 2007 9

What do you think of this book? We want to hear from you!

Microsoft is interested in hearing your feedback so we can continually improve our books and learning resources for you. To participate in a brief online survey, please visit:

www.microsoft.com/learning/booksurvey/

7   Customizing Tables   71

8   Creating Forms   87

9   Creating Queries   101

10

Creating Reports 125

11

Beautifying Forms and Reports 143

12

Creating Charts in Access 169

13 Interacting with Other Programs   179

14 Administering a Database   219

15 Customizing Access   231

16 Presenting Table and Query Data Dynamically   247

What do you think of this book? We want to hear from you!

Microsoft is interested in hearing your feedback so we can continually improve our books and learning resources for you. To participate in a brief online survey, please visit:

www.microsoft.com/learning/booksurvey/

Acknowledgments

I'm thrilled every time I get the chance to write a book for Microsoft Learning. Thanks go to Kathleen Atkins, Juliana Aldous-Atkinson, Sandra Haynes, and Lucinda Rowley for their support, trust, and faith in my efforts.

My sincere thanks also go out to Debbie Abshier, the principal of Abshier House, and Debbie Berman, Joell Smith-Borne, Kelly Dobbs Henthorne, Joyce Nielsen, and Sharon Hilgenberg, all of whom turned my words into a book. It's a lot harder than it looks, and it takes a team of professionals who love what they're doing to make it happen.

Neil Salkind, my agent, represents both myself and Studio B with aplomb. He's represented me for ten years, and I'm continually amazed at how much he gets done every day.

I'd like to thank the folks of ComedySportz Portland, led by Pat Short. Improvisational comedy provides both an excellent preparation for and release from the pressures of writing.

Finally, I'd like to thank my family. My wife Virginia provides emotional support when I need it, demonstrates the work ethic of a former professional ballerina when I need it, and is always there when I need it. My brother Doug, father David, and mother Jane have all contributed to my success. Being able to write professionally, and make a good living doing it, means more to me than they'll ever know.

1

Introduction: About This Book

If you want to get the most from your computer and your software with the least amount of time and effort—and who doesn't?—this book is for you. You'll find *Microsoft Office Access 2007 Plain & Simple* to be a straightforward, easy-to-read reference tool. With the premise that your computer should work for you, not you for it, this book's purpose is to help you get your work done quickly and efficiently so that you can get away from the computer and live your life.

No Computerese!

Let's face it: when there's a task you don't know how to do but you need to get it done in a hurry, or when you're stuck in the middle of a task and can't figure out what to do next, there's nothing more frustrating than having to read page after page of technical background material. You want the information you need—nothing more, nothing less—and you want it now! It should be easy to find and understand.

That's what this book is all about. It's written in plain English—no jargon. There's no single task in the book that takes more than a couple pages. Just look up the task in the index or the table of contents, turn to the page, and the information you need is laid out in an illustrated step-by-step format. You don't get bogged down by the whys and wherefores: Just follow the steps and get your work done.

Occasionally, you might have to turn to another page if the procedure you're working on is accompanied by a "See Also." That's because a lot of tasks overlap, and I didn't want to keep repeating myself. Some useful Tips are scattered here and there, and a "Try This" or a "Caution" is thrown in once in a while, but by and large I've tried to remain true to the heart and soul of a "Plain & Simple" book, which is that the information you need is available to you at a glance.

Useful Tasks...

Whether you use Microsoft Access 2007 at home or on the road, I've tried to pack this book with procedures for everything I could think of that you might want to do, from the simplest tasks to some of the more esoteric ones.

...And the Easiest Way to Do Them

Another thing I've tried to do in this book is find and document the easiest way to accomplish a task. Access 2007 often provides a multitude of methods to accomplish a single end result—which can be daunting or delightful, depending on the way you like to work. If you tend to stick with one favorite and familiar approach, I think the methods described in this book are the way to go. If you like trying out alternative techniques, go ahead! The intuitiveness of Access 2007 invites exploration, and you're likely to discover ways of doing things that you think are easier or that you like better than mine. If you do, that's great! It's exactly what the developers of Access had in mind when they provided so many alternatives.

A Quick Overview

Your computer probably came with Access 2007 preinstalled, but if you have to install it yourself, the setup routine makes installation so simple that you won't need my help anyway. So, unlike many computer books, this one doesn't start with installation instructions and a list of system requirements.

Next, you don't need to read this book in any particular order. You can jump in, get the information you need, and then close the book and keep it near your computer until the next time you need to know how to get something done. But that doesn't mean the information is scattered about with wild abandon. The book is organized so that the tasks you want to accomplish are arranged in two levels—you'll find the general type of task you're looking for under a main section title such as "Creating a New Database," "Getting Help," "Exporting Data to a Text File," and so on. Then, in each of those sections, the smaller tasks within the main task are arranged in a loose progression from the simplest to the more complex.

Section 1, which you're reading now, introduces *Microsoft Office Access 2007 Plain & Simple* and tells you what to expect in this book. Section 2 covers what's new in Access 2007, from the brand-new, ribbon-based user interface to the new ways you can gather Access data from your colleagues by using e-mail messages. Sections 3, 4, and 5 cover the basics of operating a database: starting Access 2007 and shutting it down, sizing and arranging program windows, getting help from within the program and on the Web, what types of objects are available in an Access database, and the role each of those objects fulfills. There's also a lot of useful information about designing and creating a new database, either from scratch or by using built-in database templates; navigating within a database; creating relationships between tables; and getting data from other Access databases.

Section 6 is all about customizing your table fields. You'll discover the different types of fields available to you; how to add, delete, and rearrange fields; and how to make data entry easier for you and your colleagues. You'll find the information helpful whether you want to change how a field displays its data, set a default value for a field, ensure the data entered into the field is appropriate for that field, or enter table data by picking the proper value from a list.

Section 7 focuses on working with entire tables, rather than individual fields in a table. Here's where you'll find information about entering data quickly, finding and replacing table text, and modifying how Access displays your data in a table. There's also a short section here on filtering a table's contents, which lets you limit the data displayed to exactly what you need to make a decision.

Sections 8 through 11 are all about building database objects to take best advantage of your data—creating forms, which let you present your data in an attractive format and enter new table records; building reports, which summarize your data and make it easy to create mailing labels; defining queries, which let you ask specific questions of your table data; and changing the appearance of your forms and reports to make them more attractive or to conform with a company's color scheme. The possibilities are endless, and I know you'll be thrilled by the flexibility, power, and ease of use of the Access 2007 tools at your disposal.

Section 12 shows you how to summarize your Access data visually by creating charts. Charts enable you to summarize large data collections quickly, compare historical data to current trends, and provide context for when you discuss specific data points from your tables. Section 13 is about interacting with other programs, such as by including files created in other programs in your databases, adding pictures to forms and reports, or including Microsoft Excel charts in your database.

You will also find out how to exchange data with other programs, whether that means exporting Access table or query data to another program or reading data from another program's files into Access.

The final sections, 14 through 16, deal with more advanced topics: sharing database data on the Web; administering your database so you can, if necessary, identify the data that is open for anyone to look over and separate that data from tables or queries that might contain more sensitive information; setting up switchboards that make it easier to move around in your databases; customizing Access by changing the items that appear on the program's Quick Access Toolbar; creating macros that automate repetitive or lengthy tasks; and creating forms that let you dynamically reorganize your data. If you think these tasks sound complex, rest assured they're not—Access 2007 makes them so easy that you'll sail right through.

A Few Assumptions

I had to make a few educated guesses about the audience when I started writing this book. Perhaps you just use Access for personal reasons—keeping track of your books, music, contacts, and so on. Perhaps you use Access at work to maintain records of your inventory, customers, and the orders they place. Or maybe you run a small home-based business. Taking all these possibilities into account, I assumed that you'd need to know how to create, modify, and work with all of the basic Access database objects; to administer the database; and to share the data on the Internet or over your company's internal network.

Another assumption I made is that you have an inherent curiosity about what you can do with Access 2007. Rather than show you how to perform specific tasks, such as designing a database to track client interactions or customer orders, I assumed you wanted a broad base of experience from which to work. I hope that the tasks in this book give a solid foundation for you to learn more about Access and what it can do for you.

A Final Word (or Two)

I had three goals in writing this book:

- Whatever you want to do, I want the book to help you get it done.

- I want the book to help you discover how to do things you *didn't* know you wanted to do.

- And, finally, if I've achieved the first two goals, I'll be well on the way to the third, which is for my book to help you *enjoy* using Access 2007. I think that's the best gift I could give you to thank you for buying my book.

I hope you'll have as much fun reading and using *Microsoft Office Access 2007 Plain & Simple* as I've had writing it. The best way to learn is by *doing,* and that's how I hope you'll use this book.

Jump right in!

What's New in Access 2007

One of the first things you'll notice about Microsoft Office Access 2007 is that the user interface has changed quite a bit. Earlier versions of Access had hundreds of commands scattered among the program's menus and toolbars; what's more, some useful commands didn't appear on any of the menus or toolbars! In Access 2007, there is only one place to look for the tools you need to use Access: the ribbon. If you've used previous versions of Access, you'll only need to spend a little bit of time working with the new user interface to use Access skillfully. If you're new to Access, you'll have a much easier time learning to use the program than you would have with the older user interface.

This section of the book introduces many of the new features in Access 2007: the new user interface and especially the ribbon; the improved formatting capabilities provided by galleries and the Mini toolbar; the new types of fields you can use in database tables; the new file format; and new data collection capabilities.

All of these improvements combine to make Access 2007 a friendly yet powerful program you can use effectively right out of the box, with a little help from *Microsoft Office Access 2007 Plain & Simple*.

Familiarizing Yourself with the New User Interface

The most obvious change to the user interface is the ribbon, which replaces all the menus and toolbars you may be familiar with. Once you've created a database, you can create new objects, format existing objects, and manage your database using the commands on the ribbon. Unlike previous versions of Access, which made you hunt through a complex toolbar and menu system to find the commands you wanted, everything you want to do can now be found in one place.

The Access 2007 ribbon divides its commands into tabs. Which tabs appear depends on what you are working on in the program, but the basic default set includes four: Home, Create, External Data, and Database Tools. The following graphic shows the ribbon's Home tab, which contains many frequently used editing and formatting functions.

The Home tab contains a series of groups: Views, Clipboard, Font, Rich Text, Records, Sort & Filter, and Find. Each group, in turn, hosts a series of controls that enable you to perform tasks related to that group (formatting fonts, filtering records, finding data, and so on). Clicking a control with a downward-pointing arrow displays a menu or palette that contains further options; if an option has an ellipses (...) after the item's name, clicking the item displays a dialog box. You can also open a dialog box by clicking the Dialog Box Launcher control at the bottom-right corner of a group; the control looks like a square that contains an arrow pointing down and to the right.

If you want to save your database under a new name or in a new location, close the active database, print one or more database objects, or change some of the program's settings, click the Microsoft Office button at the top left corner of the Access 2007 program window.

Formatting Database Objects Using New AutoFormats

Access has always been a powerful program that you could use to manage your data effectively, but the built-in formats you could use to style your forms and reports didn't inspire graphic artists to greater heights. Sure, you could change the forms and reports by hand if you wanted to, but it took a fair amount of work, and it wasn't as easy as applying an existing theme.

I'm happy to say that your wait for attractive built-in AutoFormat themes is over. Access 2007 comes with a series of AutoFormats you can apply to make your forms and reports look the way you want them to. What's more, if you're artistically inclined, you can create your own AutoFormats so you only need to make your formatting changes once. After you save your designs as an AutoFormat, all you need to do is select the AutoFormat from the list of available formats and apply it with a few mouse clicks.

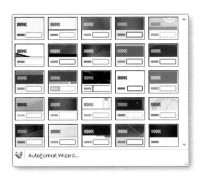

Creating New Types of Fields

General database functions, such as storing data in tables, finding specific data by using queries, and displaying data in forms and reports, are fairly well defined and have been for some time. The types of data traditionally stored in database tables are text values, numbers, dates, and so on. As time has passed and computers have become faster and more powerful, users' needs have changed. Product databases, for example, benefit from having pictures of the products stored in the database. Yes, in previous versions of Access you could link to a file by using a hyperlink or OLE data type, but Access 2007 cuts to the chase and lets you include the image in your database directly.

If you like, you can attach multiple images to a product record by creating a multivalued field—that is, a field that can contain more than one image, description, department code, or whatever. One easy way to think of how multivalued fields could be useful is in a university setting where one class is part of two departments' curricula. (History 302 is the same class as English 412, for example.)

Finally, Access 2007 allows you to define a Memo field that is append-only, where users are only able to add new information to the field; they can neither delete nor edit any data already entered into the field. Append-only Memo fields are useful for test results, price quotes, and other circumstances where it's essential that you keep an accurate, unchanging record of information that has been entered into the field.

Collecting Data from E-mail Messages

In many companies, getting employees to fill out expense vouchers, contact reports, educational expense reimbursement forms, purchase requests, and surveys is a nightmare that eats up a lot more of your time than it should. If your employees create a paper form that someone has to reenter into a database, you're doubling the work required for a simple operation and greatly increasing the potential for error. If an employee fills out a form in a third-party application that lets you import the data into Access, you've added unnecessary steps to the process.

In the 2007 Microsoft Office system, you can avoid all of the problems of paper forms by sending forms to your colleagues through your e-mail system. You can choose to send Hypertext Markup Language (HTML) forms like the one shown that can be read by most e-mail systems, including Outlook 2007, or, if both you and your recipients have InfoPath 2007 installed, you can send an InfoPath 2007 form for them to fill out. After your colleagues fill out the forms in their e-mail programs or InfoPath, they return it to you. Then, from either Outlook or InfoPath, you can download the data directly into the table you used to create the form. It really is just that simple.

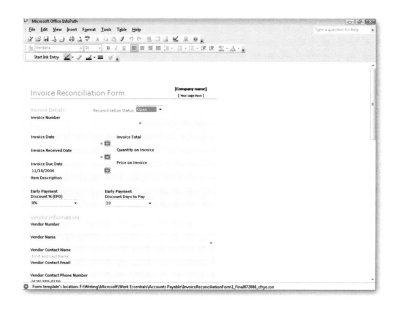

3

Introducing Access 2007

Microsoft Office Access 2007 is designed to help you store, combine, and ask questions of large collections of data relevant to your business or your home life. You can create databases to track products and sales for a garden supply company, or, just as easily, build databases to keep track of your books and holiday card lists. Regardless of the specific use you have in mind, Access is a versatile program you can use to store and retrieve data quickly.

Working with Access is pretty straightforward. The program has a number of templates you can use to create entire databases or just parts of them. You also have the freedom to create databases and their components from scratch, giving you the flexibility you need to build any database.

This section of the book covers the basics: what a database is and how it works, starting Access, shutting it down, opening databases, and introducing the new features in Access 2007. There's also an overall view of the Access window with labels for the most important parts of the program. You can use that image as a touchstone for learning more about Access.

Introducing Databases

Storing Data on Index Cards

Before computers, a popular way to store data was on index cards. If you ran a gardening supply store, you could keep track of your products by creating a card for each product, dividing the cards into product categories, and then alphabetizing the cards in each section by product name. Each card would contain relevant data such as the product's name, unique identifier, category, price, description, and the supplier's name and phone number.

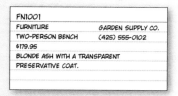

To find all of the products from a specific supplier, you either needed to keep track of the products on a separate sheet of paper or go through the cards and pull every one representing a product made by that supplier.

Storing Data on the Computer

If you store the same data on the computer, however, you can find all of the products from a specific supplier much more easily. As an example, you might create a Microsoft Word table with a column for each type of data you want to store.

With the list in a Word table, you can change the order of the table rows to group all of the products from one supplier together...all you need to do then is scroll down through the table until you find the products from the supplier you want.

Using Word to store your data isn't the best solution, however. One limitation is that there's no way to combine information from two tables, so you need to write the supplier's phone number in every row representing a product from that supplier. If that phone number changes, you need to change the phone number entry in every table row representing a product from that supplier.

Storing Data in a Database

Databases, by contrast, are designed to combine data from several sources into a single table. Once data is entered into a table, it can be combined with other tables in the database to produce valuable information. It's possible, for example, to store information about suppliers in one table and information about purchase orders in another table. If a supplier changes its phone number, you need to change the phone number only once.

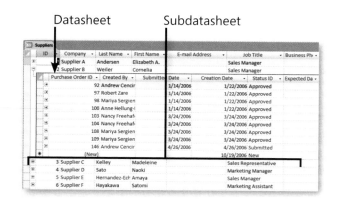

Starting Access

After you install Access on your computer, you can run it to create new databases or to work with existing databases. There are two easy ways to run Access—you can start it from the Start menu or by double-clicking a shortcut on your desktop. Regardless of the method you choose, you end up with the power of an Access database at your fingertips in the few seconds it takes your computer to start the program.

Start Access

1. Click the Start button on the Taskbar.
2. Click All Programs.
3. Click Microsoft Office.
4. Click Microsoft Office Access 2007.

Create a Shortcut for Access

1. Click the Start button on the Taskbar.
2. Click All Programs.
3. Click Microsoft Office.
4. Right-click Microsoft Office Access 2007.
5. Point to Send To.
6. Click Desktop (create shortcut).
7. Press the Escape key twice to close the menu.

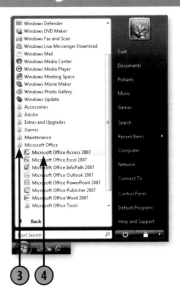

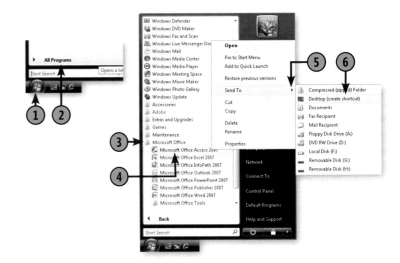

Tip

You can rename a shortcut by right-clicking it, clicking Rename on the shortcut menu that appears, typing a new name for the shortcut, and pressing Enter.

Surveying the Access Window

- The title bar displays the name of the database and the window control buttons.

- The tabs on the ribbon enable you to display different types of commands based on the category you select.

- The ribbon contains commands that reflect the active Contextual tab, your position in the database, and the selected objects.

- The Navigation pane displays database objects of the type you select.

- The object window displays any open database objects.

- The status bar indicates the progress of any ongoing processes.

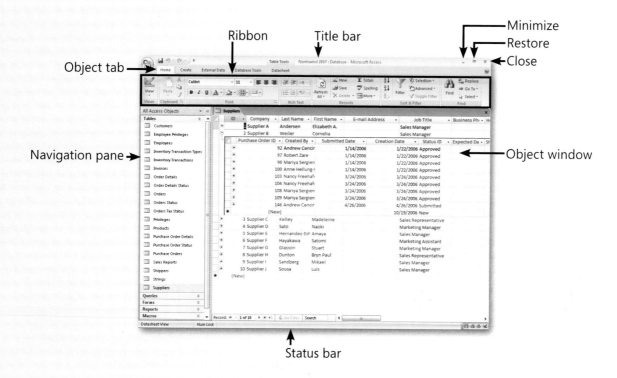

Ribbon

Title bar

Minimize

Restore

Close

Object tab

Navigation pane

Object window

Status bar

Opening a Database

When you start Access, the Getting Started with Microsoft Office Access screen appears in the Access window. A list of recently opened files appears at the right of the window, in the Open Recent Database section. You can select the file you want to open from the list that appears. If the file you want isn't on that list, click More to display the Open dialog box. From the Open dialog box, you can navigate to the folder with the database you want to open.

Open a Database on Start-up

1. Start Microsoft Office Access 2007.
2. Click More.
3. Navigate to the folder with the database you want to open.
4. Double-click the file you want to open.

Open a Recently Used Database

1. Start Microsoft Office Access 2007.
2. In the Open Recent Database section, click the name of the database you want to open.

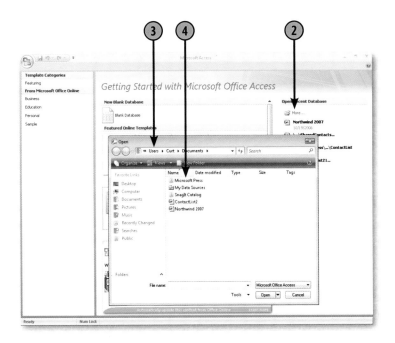

Viewing Multiple Database Objects

Microsoft Office Access 2007 enables you to work with multiple database objects more efficiently than in previous versions of the program. In Access 2007, the program displays a tab representing each open object at the top of the object window. If you want to display an object that is currently hidden, you can click that object's tab to display it. When you display an object in the object window, you can close the object by clicking its Close button (located at the top right corner of the object window).

Close a Database Object

① Click the Close button to close the displayed database object.

Scroll within a Database Object

■ Click the up or down arrow on the vertical scroll bar to scroll up and down within the object.

■ Click the left or right arrow on the horizontal scroll bar to scroll left or right within the object.

Tip

If you would prefer to have Access display database objects in the same manner that Windows Vista displays program windows (with maximize, minimize, and close buttons), click the Microsoft Office button and then click Access Options. In the Access Options dialog box, on the Current Database tab, select the Overlapping Windows option button and then click OK.

Tab

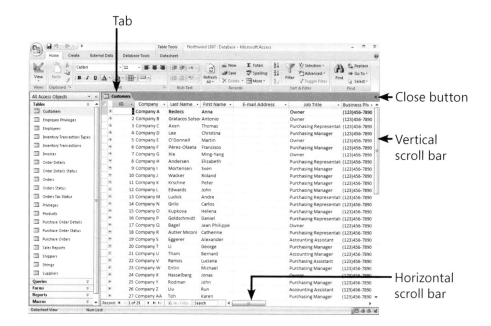

Close button

Vertical scroll bar

Horizontal scroll bar

Closing a Database and Exiting Access

When you finish working with an Access database, close it to free up system resources and let your computer run other programs more quickly. By the same token, after you complete all the work you need to do in Access, you should exit the program entirely. If you work in a corporate environment, or if your database contains sensitive information such as client addresses or account numbers, you should always close your database any time you walk away from your computer. Although it's unlikely that someone will wander by and copy or write down sensitive information, it's better that you make it as difficult as possible for anyone with bad intentions to make off with your data.

Close a Database

① Click the Microsoft Office button.

② Click Close Database.

Tip

If you finish working with the current database and want to open another, save your work (if necessary), click the Office button, and then click Open.

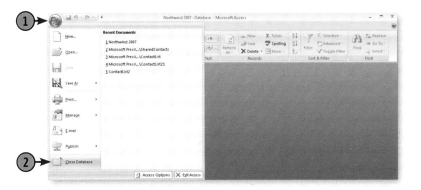

Caution

Clicking the Close button at the top right corner of the Access window will exit Access, not just close the active database.

Exit Access

① Click the Microsoft Office button.

② Click Exit Access.

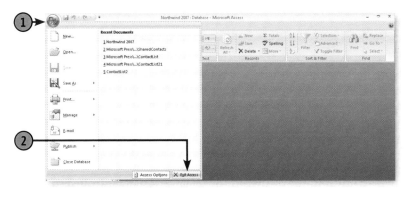

Displaying and Managing Database Objects

Access databases typically contain lots of objects: tables, where you store your data; forms, which enable you to enter data into tables quickly; queries, which enable you to extract subsets of data from your tables; and reports, which summarize your table data and query results. Access organizes your objects in the Navigation pane, found at the left edge of the program window. You can choose the order in which Access displays the objects and even choose whether to display a subset of your objects, but you always know where your objects are if you want them. The Shutter Bar, located at the top of the Navigation pane, enables you to select how you want to view your database's objects. If you want to maximize the size of the object window, you can hide the Shutter Bar.

When you have more than one database object open, Access represents the objects as a series of tabs across the top of the database window. All you have to do to display an object is click its tab, and closing an object is as simple as clicking the Close button at the top-right corner of the object's window.

Open a Database Object

1 If necessary, click the Shutter Bar Open/Close button to display the Navigation pane.

2 Click the Shutter Bar.

3 If there's no check mark next to All Access Objects, click All Access Objects.

4 If necessary, click the Show Details button to display the objects in the desired category.

5 Double-click the object you want to open.

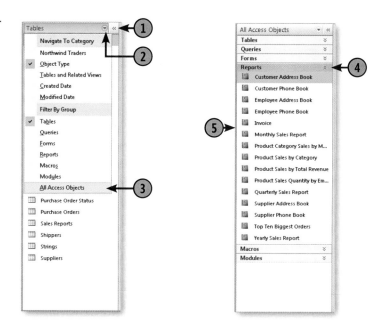

Control Object Display in the Navigation Pane

1 If necessary, click the Shutter Bar Open/Close Button to display the Navigation pane.

2 Click the Shutter Bar.

3 Follow one of these steps:

- Select Tables and Related Views to display only your data tables and views.

- Select Object Type to display all of the objects in your database, sorted by object type.

- Select Created Date to display all of the objects in your database, sorted by the date the objects were created.

- Select Modified Date to display all of the objects in your database, sorted by the date the objects were last changed.

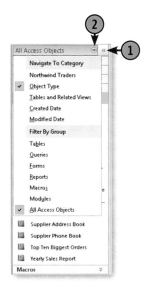

Using the Access Help System

If you need to get help using Access, there are a number of places you can look. One option is to right-click an object (such as a database object or a graphic) to see a list of things you can do with the object. You can also open the Access Help files and browse through them to find the answer to a specific question or just to explore.

Get Suggested Commands from Shortcut Menus

1 Right-click any Access object to see the shortcut menu of commands.

2 Click a command.

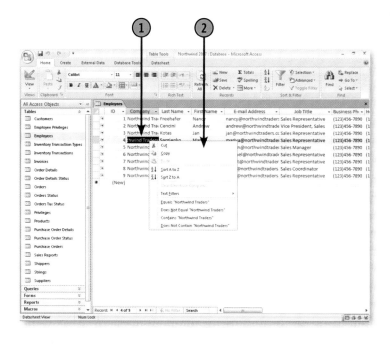

Get Microsoft Access Help

① Click the Microsoft Access Help button on the ribbon.

Get Help on the Web

① Click the Microsoft Access Help button on the ribbon.

② Click the Search button's down arrow, and select where you want to look for help.

③ Type your search terms.

④ Click the Search button.

⑤ Browse the topics displayed for help and resources.

Tip

You can visit the Microsoft Office Assistance Center site directly by opening your Web browser and typing *http://office.microsoft.com/assistance/* in the Address box.

Tip

If you use Access at work, you should definitely visit the Microsoft Office Online Work Essentials site at *http://office.microsoft.com/en-us/FX010931361033.aspx.* The Work Essentials site is organized by occupation and by task, so you should have no trouble finding articles and demonstrations that can help you get your work done quickly.

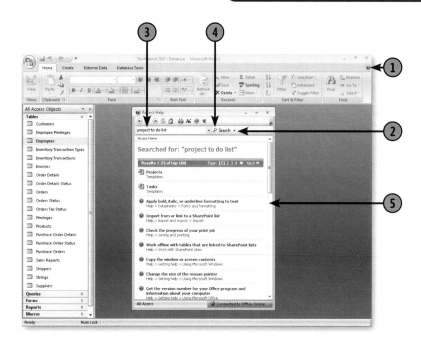

4

Getting to Know Access Databases

Microsoft Office Access 2007 is a powerful program with a wide variety of objects you can create to manage, locate, and present important information. The best way to get familiar with Access and what you can do with it is to dive right in by examining a sample database. Access 2007 comes with the Northwind sample database, which chronicles the activities and resources of a food and beverage dealer. In addition to the Northwind sample database, Access also comes with several database templates you can use to create databases to track your business assets, contacts, issues, projects, and other tasks.

Each object type has a definite role in the functioning of the database. Tables are the building block of your collection—that's where the data is stored. You can ask questions about your data by creating queries, present the data one record at a time in forms, or group records by their contents in reports. One type of form is the switchboard, which has controls you can click to open popular database objects, organizes your database contents onto switchboard pages, and even lets you exit Access by clicking a form button.

This section introduces the database elements you use most often, explains the elements of each object type, and shows you how to create your own database using a wizard.

Viewing a Sample Database

One of the best ways to get a feel for using Access is to work with an existing database. The Northwind database, which you install along with Access, is a complete database with tables, queries, reports, and forms you can examine to see what goes into a solid database design.

Open a Sample Database

1. Start Access 2007.
2. Click Sample.
3. Click Northwind 2007.
4. Click Download.
5. Click Login to start the database.

Tip

The Northwind database contains a form, which appears when you open the database, that enables you to log in using different user accounts. If a database you create doesn't use such a screen, you won't have to log in to use the file.

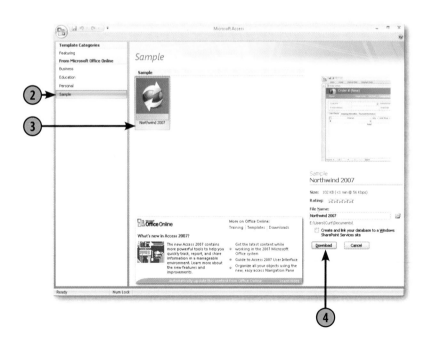

Working with Database Objects

Every element of a database, be it a table, form, report, or query, is represented in the Access window as an object. This section shows you how to display a category of objects, open an individual object for viewing, and open an object for editing. Future sections go into more detail about what you can do with each type of object.

Display a Class of Objects

① If necessary, click the Shutter Bar.

② Select the name of the object class to display.

Open an Object

① Double-click the target object.

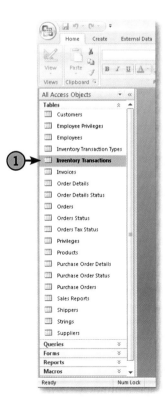

View an Object in Design View

① Right-click the target object.

② Click Design View.

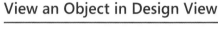
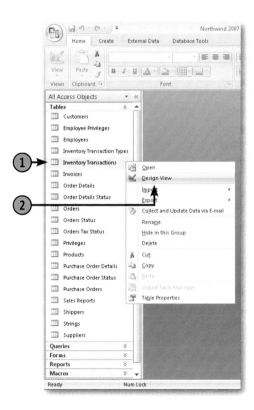

Save an Object

■ Click the Save button.

Delete an Object

① Click an object.

② Click the Home tab.

③ In the Records group, click the Delete button.

④ In the dialog box that appears, click Yes to confirm that you want to delete the object.

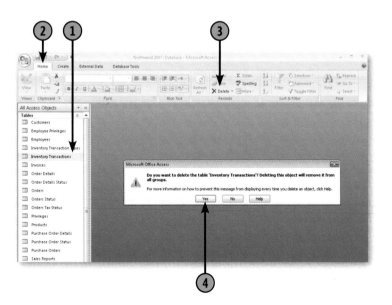

Examining a Table

The basic building block of a database is the table, which is where you store your data. Tables are made up of columns (also called *fields*) and rows (also called *records*). A field holds a particular type of data, such as a name or phone number, while a record has a complete set of fields relating to an entity (such as a person's name, address, and phone number).

View a Table

① If necessary, click the Shutter Bar Open/Close button.

② Click the Shutter Bar.

③ Click Tables.

④ Double-click a table.

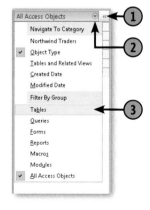

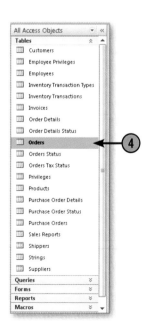

Navigate in a Table

- Press Tab to move to the next cell.

- Press Shift+Tab to move to the previous cell.

- Press Home to move to the first cell of the first row.

- Press End to move to the last cell of the active row.

- Drag the vertical scroll box up or down to view table rows not currently displayed.

- Drag the horizontal scroll box to the left or right to view fields not currently displayed.

- Use the controls on the record navigation bar to move among records.

Tip

You can get a complete list of keyboard shortcuts in Access by pressing F1 to display the Help window, typing **keyboard shortcuts** in the search box, and clicking the Search button.

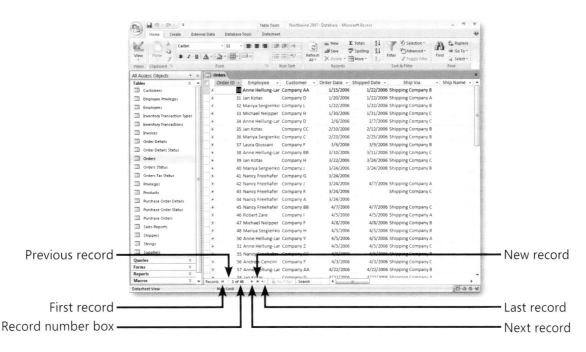

Previous record

New record

First record

Last record

Record number box

Next record

Examining a Form

Forms are database objects that make it easier for you to view data stored in tables or retrieved by queries. Rather than present the data in a compact grid, creating forms to display table and query data lets you arrange fields on the form and add explanatory text to help you and your colleagues understand the form's contents. You can also enter new records into a table through a form.

View a Form

① If necessary, click the Shutter Bar Open/Close Button.

② Click the Shutter Bar.

③ Click Forms.

④ Double-click a form.

Enter Data Using a Form

① Click the New Record button.

② Type your data in the first field and press Tab.

③ Continue entering data. When you enter data in the last field and press Tab, Access creates a new record.

Caution

If you don't enter data in the last field, Access may not write your data to the table. You can save your work in progress by clicking the Save button.

Tip

As in a table, you can use the navigation bar at the bottom left of the form window to move among the form records, or if the form is based on a table, to enter a new record.

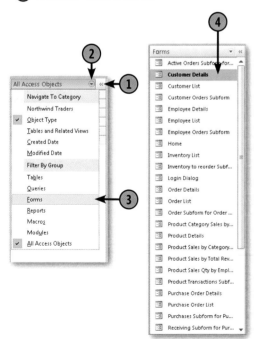

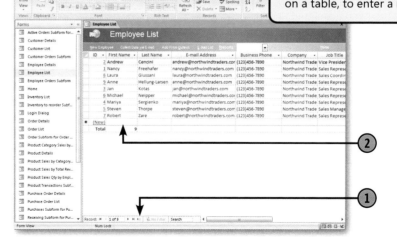

Navigating Using a Switchboard

When you create a database with a lot of tables, queries, and forms, it can be hard for your colleagues to recognize which objects hold which information. You can make their job easier by creating a switchboard with the most important objects on the front page. The usual name for the switchboard that appears when a database opens is Main Switchboard, but you can name your switchboard form anything you want.

Open a Switchboard

① If necessary, click the Shutter Bar Open/Close Button.

② Click the Shutter Bar.

③ Click Forms.

④ Double-click Switchboard.

Move Using a Switchboard

① Click a switchboard control.

② Click the Close button to close the switchboard page.

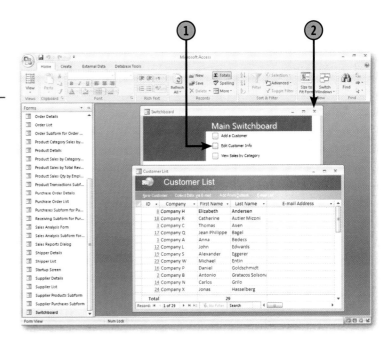

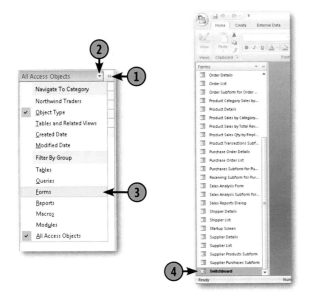

See Also

For information on creating switchboards of your own, see "Creating a Switchboard" on page 225.

Examining a Query

When a table has just a few rows, it's easy to scroll through it to find a few records with the data you want. For larger tables, though, you can create queries to find records that meet a criteria, such as orders from a particular customer. This type of query is known as a select query. Access enables you to create quite a few other types of queries, including queries that create new tables from the query's results, find duplicate records, or update the values in a table.

View a Query

① If necessary, click the Shutter Bar Open/Close Button.

② Click the Shutter Bar.

③ Click Queries.

④ Double-click a query.

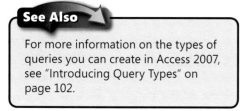

See Also

For more information on the types of queries you can create in Access 2007, see "Introducing Query Types" on page 102.

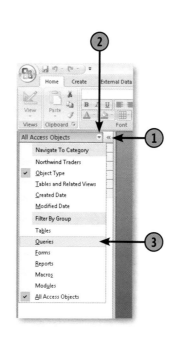

Examining a Report

Access usually presents your tables and query results in datasheets that display your data in a compact but not very easy-to-read format. You can make your data easier to read by displaying it in forms, but forms only display one record at a time. Reports, by contrast, can show more than one record on the same page. A report also enables you to sort and group the records it displays to show all products in a given category before moving on to the products in the next category.

View a Report

① If necessary, click the Shutter Bar Open/Close Button.

② Click the Shutter Bar.

③ Click Reports.

④ Double-click a report.

See Also

For information about grouping records, see "Grouping Report Records" on page 135.

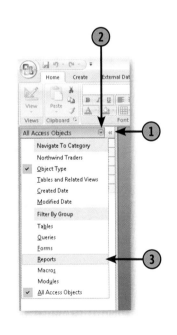

Using the Database Templates

The developers of Microsoft Office Access 2007 have one primary goal: to make it as easy as possible for you to create powerful and useful databases that help you get your work done quickly. You must have a great database program to meet that goal, but it also helps if the developers draw on the rest of the Microsoft community to design databases you can use without modification (for tasks such as tracking your contacts, sales, or workouts) or to use as the basis for your own custom databases. You can find those preexisting databases, called templates, installed on your computer and also on the Office Online Web site.

Create a Database from a Template

1. If necessary, click the Microsoft Office button and then choose Close Database to close any open database.

2. Click a Template Category.

3. Click the desired template.

4. Type a name for your database.

5. Click the folder icon.

6. Navigate to the folder where you want to store your database.

7. Click OK.

8. Click Download.

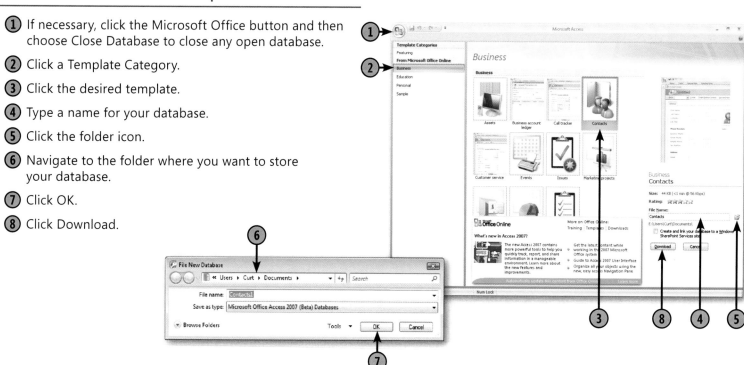

Find Database Templates Online

(1) If necessary, click the Microsoft Office button and then click Close Database to close any open database.

(2) Click an Office Online template category.

(3) Click the desired template.

(4) Type a name for your database.

(5) Click the folder icon.

(6) Navigate to the folder where you want to store your database.

(7) Click OK.

(8) Click Download.

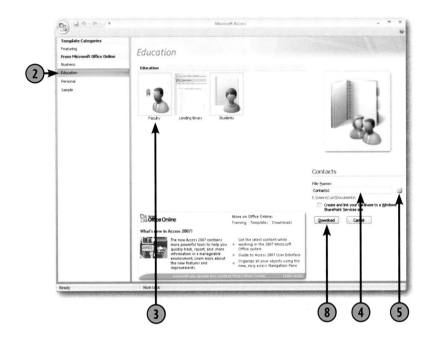

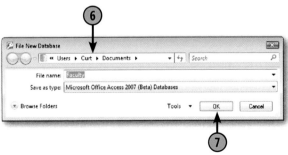

Frequently Used Object Views

Each object has a number of views, or ways of looking at and working with the object and its contents. Opening any object in Design view, for example, lets you change the object's structure and appearance. The following table has a list of the views available for each Access object type.

See Also

For more information on PivotTables and PivotCharts, see "Presenting Table and Query Data Dynamically" on page 247.

Access Object Views

Object	Views	Description
Table	Design	Opens the table so you can add, delete, or modify fields
	Datasheet	Displays the table data as rows in an unformatted worksheet
	PivotTable	Displays a PivotTable construction interface
	PivotChart	Displays a PivotTable and PivotChart construction interface
Query	Design	Opens the query so you can add, delete, or modify fields, criteria, and any actions the query takes when it runs
	Datasheet	Displays the query results as rows in an unformatted worksheet
	SQL	Displays the query's representation in the Structured Query Language (SQL)
	PivotTable	Displays a PivotTable construction interface
	PivotChart	Displays a PivotTable and PivotChart construction interface
Form	Design	Opens the form so you can add, delete, or modify fields and controls
	Form	Displays the form data using the layout you defined
	Datasheet	Displays the form data as rows in an unformatted worksheet
	Layout	Displays the form so you can change its size as well as the size and position of its headers and footers
	PivotTable	Displays a PivotTable construction interface
	PivotChart	Displays a PivotTable and PivotChart construction interface
Report	Design	Opens the report so you can add, delete, or modify fields and controls
	Report	Displays the table or query data with the formatting and organization you specified when you created the report
	Print Preview	Displays the report as it will be printed
	Layout	Displays the report so you can change its size as well as the size and position of its sections, headers, and footers

5

Creating a Database

If none of the databases you can create using one of the Access database templates meets your needs, you can create a database from scratch. When you choose to create a new table, you have complete control over the number of fields, the names of the fields, and what sort of data they can store. After you create the table, you can also add fields from the Field Templates task pane, which contains a wide variety of fields to store such data as times, dates, phone numbers, postal codes, names, addresses, and comments.

Once you create a table, whether from scratch or by using a template, you can change its structure as needed, such as renaming an existing field or adding an entirely new field to store additional data.

Designing a Database

The most basic object in a database is the table where you store your data. You might be tempted to jam every type of data you want to store into a single table, but that's hardly ever the right way to design tables in a database. The following guidelines will help you create efficient tables.

One Table Per Object

The first rule in creating database tables is to ensure every table stores data about one type of object, whether that object is a person, a product, or an order. As an example, consider the Suppliers table from the Northwind database.

This table has a field for everything you want to know about a supplier, with nothing extra. Consider this alternative design, which adds fields to describe the supplier's products.

Aside from repeated data, deleting the record representing the last product from a supplier removes all information about that supplier from your database. Rather than risk losing that information, it is much more efficient to create one table for the suppliers and another for the products.

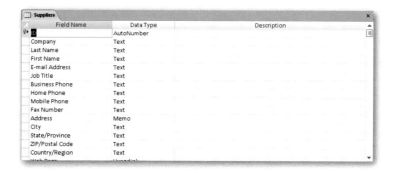

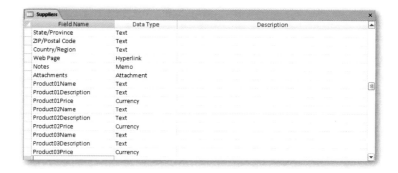

Give Every Table a Primary Key

Another important consideration in creating a table is to assign a *primary key*. This field contains a value that sets a record apart from all other records in the table. In the Northwind database's Shippers table, that role is filled by the ID field.

ID field

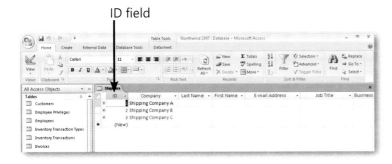

It's also possible to create a primary key made up of more than one field, as in the table shown in the following illustration. (Please note that this table is just a sample; it isn't in the Northwind database.)

The ProductID field identifies the product and the SupplierID field identifies the product's supplier. Because you can order the same product from more than one supplier, both the ProductID and SupplierID fields are needed to distinguish a record from all other records in the table.

Include Foreign Keys

A final thing you can do to make your tables more efficient is to include primary key fields from other tables, as with the SupplierIDs field in the Products table.

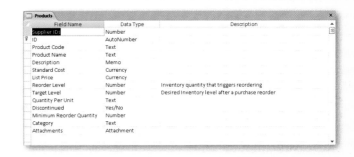

When a primary key from one table is stored in another table, it is called a *foreign key*. As you see later in this chapter, you can use foreign keys to create relationships between tables.

Creating a New Database

If you want to create a new database from scratch, you can do so by creating a blank database and then adding your own tables and other objects. You can also create a new database based on an existing database, saving yourself lots of time and effort.

Begin a New Database

1. Click the Microsoft Office button and then click New.

2. Click Blank Database.

3. Type a name for your database.

4. Click the folder icon.

5. Navigate to the folder where you want to store the database.

6. Click OK.

7. Click Create.

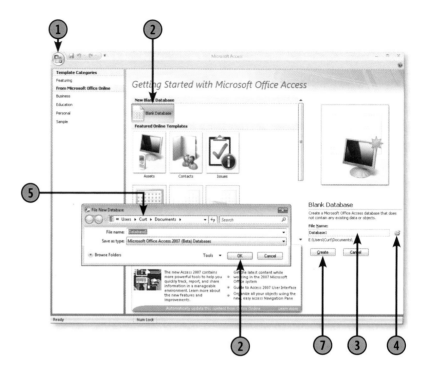

Create a New Database Based on Another Database

① Open the database you want to use as a model and then click the Microsoft Office button.

② Click the Save As menu item's arrow.

③ Click the current file format.

④ Type a different name for the new database.

⑤ Click Save.

Caution

If you don't type a new name for your database you will just save the existing database, not create a new file.

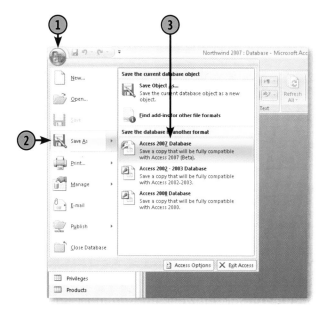

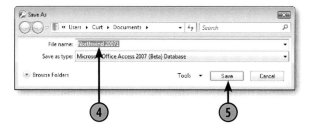

Creating a New Table in Design View

After you draw out your database on paper, you can start creating tables to store your data. One good way to define your table's structure is to start out in Design view. When you look at a table in Design view, you can define the name of a field, select the type of data to go into that field (numerical values, currency values, text, dates, phone numbers, and so on), and write a description for that field. Field descriptions are one of the most overlooked parts of database design. It's easy to overlook them or see them as unnecessary, but the reality is that you might forget what sort of data is supposed to go into a field. You could also leave the company and force someone else to figure out what a particular field should contain. If you've ever been handed someone else's database, you probably encountered a field you weren't sure about. Please make everyone's job easier by adding a description!

Create a Table in Design View

① Click the Create tab.

② In the Tables group, click Table Design.

(continued on the next page)

> **Caution**
>
> Creating a database table that doesn't include a primary key field makes it difficult to get data out of your table by using queries and in relationships with other tables. You should always have a primary key field in every table you create.

Create a Table in
Design View *(continued)*

③ Type a name for the first field and press Tab.

④ Click the Data Type down arrow.

⑤ Select a data type.

⑥ Type a description for the field.

⑦ Press Tab and repeat steps 4 through 7 to add fields.

⑧ Click the Save button.

⑨ Type a name for the table.

⑩ Click OK.

⑪ When asked whether you want Access to assign a primary key to your table, follow one of these steps:

■ Click Yes to have Access assign a primary key.

■ Click No to have Access create the table without a primary key.

■ Click Cancel to continue without saving your table.

⑫ Click the Close box for the table.

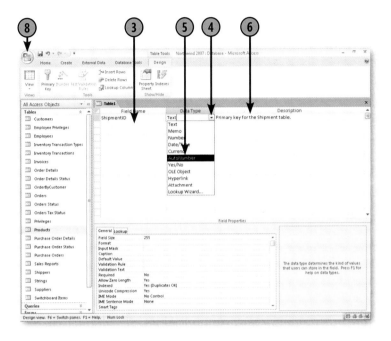

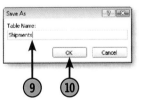

Creating a New Table by Typing

It might seem strange to want to enter data into a table without first defining the table's structure, but there's one scenario where it makes perfect sense: when you're in a hurry and you have to get the data into the database quickly. When you type data into a blank table, Access assigns generic names to the fields, such as Field1, Field2, and so on. After the data's in the table, you can open the table in Design view and name the fields, define data types, and so on.

Create a New Table by Typing

① Click the Create tab.

② In the Tables group, click Table.

③ Type the data for the first new field and press Tab.

④ Repeat step 3 until you have typed all of the data for one record, and then press Enter twice to return to the first field.

⑤ Click Save.

⑥ Type a name for your table.

⑦ Click OK.

⑧ Click the Close box for the table.

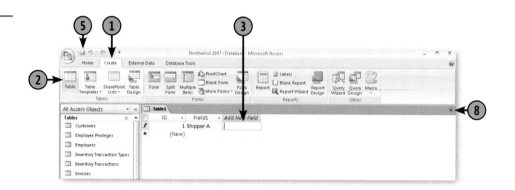

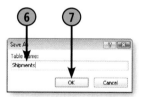

Tip

When you create a field by typing, Access defines the table's first field as a sequentially numbered field named ID, which serves as the table's primary key field. It's a good idea to leave the field in the table, but you should rename it to something more descriptive so you can identify it if you use it as a foreign key. If the table's name is Warehouses, for example, you could name the field WarehouseID.

Adding Existing Fields to a Table

Rather than force you to create a new table from scratch when you start a new database, Access lets you use the Field Templates task pane to choose commonly used fields from a number of preconstructed tables. The tables are the same tables found when you click the Table Templates button on the Create tab, but they contain a wide variety of fields that enable you to flesh out your tables with a minimum of effort. You can also copy fields from existing tables into your new table. When you click the Add Existing Fields button, Access displays the Field List task pane, which contains the structure of your existing tables and lets you copy those fields into your tables.

Add Fields from the Field Templates Task Pane

① Open a table in Datasheet view.

② Click the Datasheet contextual tab.

③ Click New Field.

④ Click the field you want to add.

⑤ Drag the field to the desired location in your datasheet.

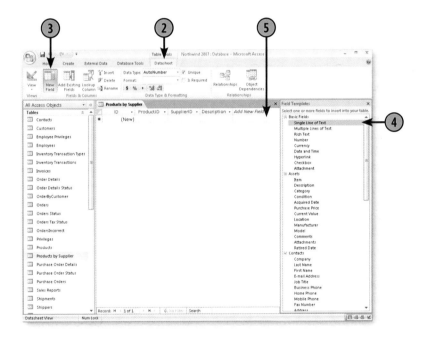

Add Fields from Existing Tables

① Open a table in Datasheet view.

② Click the Datasheet contextual tab.

③ Click Add Existing Fields.

④ Click the Show Detail control next to the desired table.

⑤ Drag the field to the desired location in your datasheet.

⑥ Click Next twice and then click Finish to close the Lookup Wizard and add the field.

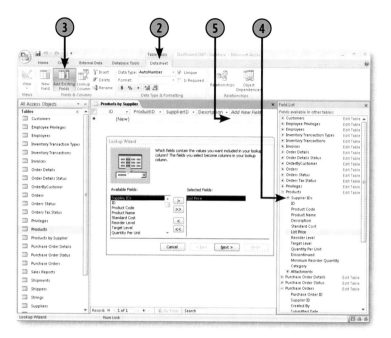

Tip ✔

When you add a field from the Field Templates task pane, drag the field name to the header row at the top of the datasheet. A vertical line appears when the field is in position to be dropped in the table; the line indicates where the new field will appear in the datasheet.

Caution !

When you add fields from the Field Templates task pane or another table, sometimes a field you add doesn't appear in your datasheet. Don't worry — it's there, but you can't see it. That's because Access hides fields that it determines could be part of your table's primary key. You can display all of your table's fields by opening the table in Datasheet view, right-clicking one of the field names, choosing Unhide Columns, selecting the check box next to the fields you want to display, and clicking Close.

Setting a Primary Key

One aspect of sound table design is to have a field (or group of fields) with a value unique to each row in the table. The fields that have the unique value are called the *primary key* field(s). Because each row's primary key field (or fields) contains a unique value, Access can distinguish each row from all of the other rows in the table. Why is that important? Consider what

would happen if a store used your phone number to identify you when you called in to place an order. If you change phone numbers and the next person assigned your phone number calls in before you do, the store replaces your information with the new caller's, potentially wiping out any record you had of doing business with the store.

Assign a Primary Key

① If necessary, click the Shutter Bar Open/Close Button.

② Click the Shutter Bar.

③ Click Tables.

④ Right-click the desired table.

⑤ Click Design View.

⑥ Click the row selector of the field to be the primary key.

⑦ Make sure the Design tab is open, and click the Primary Key button.

⑧ Click the Save button to save your work.

⑨ Click the Close box.

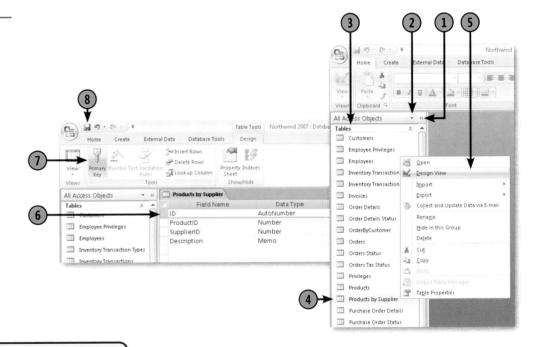

Tip

The primary key shouldn't contain meaningful information. The best value for a primary key field is a number that Access increments for each row in a table. That type of field is called an AutoNumber field.

Tip

You can create a multiple-field primary key by Ctrl clicking the row selectors of the fields to be in the primary key.

Getting Data from Other Access Tables

Many times you find that data from another database would be nice to have in the database you're working on. You can bring tables (or other objects) into your database using the controls on the External Data tab. Copying tables from another database enables you to use the data as it exists at the time you make the copy, so any updates you make to the original table are not reflected in the copy, and vice versa.

Copy a Table from Another Database

① Click the External Data tab.

② Click Access.

③ Click Browse.

④ Double-click the database from which you want to import the table.

(continued on the next page)

Tip

You can import data from other types of database objects by clicking the object type (for example, Queries) in the Import Objects dialog box and then clicking the object from which you want to get your data.

Copy a Table from Another Database (continued)

⑤ Select the Import Tables, Queries, Forms, Reports, Macros, and Modules into the Current Database option.

⑥ Click OK.

⑦ Click the table or tables to import.

⑧ Click OK.

See Also

For information on linking to a table instead of copying it, see "Linking to a Table in Another Access Database" on page 192.

Tip

If you clicked a table to include it in the list of tables to be imported, but have changed your mind, you can click the table again to deselect it.

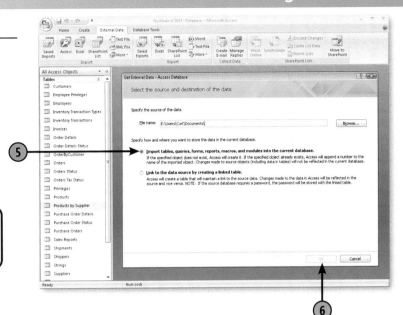

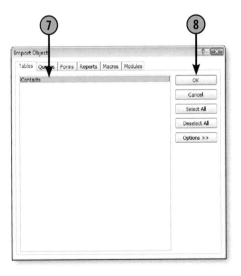

Relationships Explained

One-to-Many Relationships

One of the strengths of Access is the ability to create relationships between tables. As an example of a relationship, consider the Customers and Orders tables from the Northwind sample database.

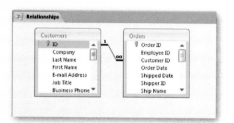

In the Northwind business case, every order comes from a single customer. Of course, a customer can place more than one order, which means that the Customers and Orders tables are in a one-to-many relationship with the Customers table on the "one" side and the Orders table on the "many" side.

Many-to-Many Relationships

It is also possible for two tables to be in a *many-to-many* relationship, where multiple records from one table relate to multiple records from another table. As an example, consider the Products and Orders tables in the Northwind database: A product can be included in many orders, and an order can include many products. The problem is that you can't relate the two tables directly without adding fields to the Orders table to hold spots for more than one item, as in the following incorrect example.

This table is poorly designed because it forces you to enter data about the customer and the order in each record, instead of just once, and that an order can't be for more items than you have spots in the table. The proper way to manage the relationship is to create a *transition table*, which bridges the gap between the Products and Orders tables. In the Northwind database, the Order Details table is a transition table.

The Order Details table is on the "many" side of two one-to-many relationships—the first with the Products table and the second with the Orders table. By bridging the two tables, it lets you manage the relationship between the Orders and Products tables without resorting to improper table design.

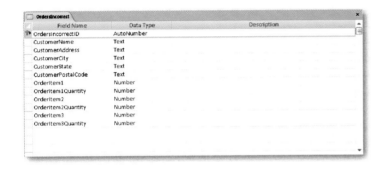

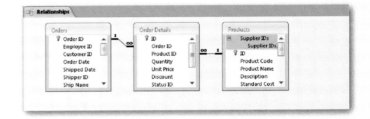

Creating Relationships between Tables

When the primary key from one table is present in another table, you can create a relationship between the two tables. This ability to link two (or more) tables together is one reason why relational databases are so powerful—you make your data easier to read by creating simple tables and then use your computer's processing power to combine tables of data into useful information you can use to make business decisions.

Define a Relationship

1. Click the Database Tools tab.
2. Click Relationships.
3. If one or more of the tables you want to relate don't appear in the Relationships window, click the Show Table button.
4. Click the first table to add to the Relationships window.
5. Click Add.
6. Repeat steps 4 and 5 as necessary.
7. When you finish adding tables, click Close.

(continued on the next page)

Tip

To delete a table from the Relationships window, right-click the table's title bar and then click Hide Table.

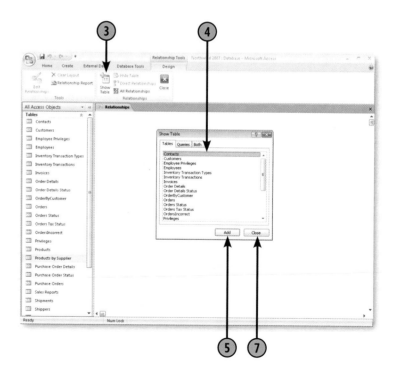

Define a Relationship *(continued)*

⑧ Drag the primary key field from the first table to the corresponding foreign key field in the second table.

⑨ Click Create.

⑩ Click the Close button to close the Relationships window.

Tip ✓

The foreign key field and the primary key field don't have to have the same name, they just need to denote the same data.

Caution !

It is possible to add a table more than once—make sure you click the name of the table you want to add! Nothing bad happens, but you won't have added the tables you want to work with.

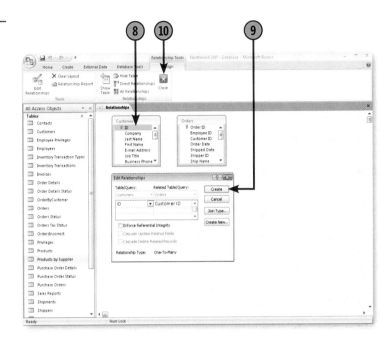

Enforcing Referential Integrity

When you create a relationship between two tables, you need to make sure that data in the two tables remains consistent. If you no longer order from a supplier, you would want all prod- ucts from that supplier deleted from the Products table when you delete the supplier's data from the Suppliers table. Enforc- ing referential integrity lets you do that.

Enforce Referential Integrity

① Click the Database Tools tab.

② Click Relationships.

③ Double-click the line representing the relationship you want to edit.

④ Select the Enforce Referential Integrity check box.

- ■ Selecting the Cascade Update Related Fields check box means Access will change the values in foreign key fields when the corresponding primary key field's value is changed.

- ■ Selecting the Cascade Delete Related Records check box means that deleting a record from the primary field in a relationship will cause Access to delete all related records in the second table.

⑤ Click OK.

⑥ Click the Save button.

⑦ Click the Close box of the Relationships window.

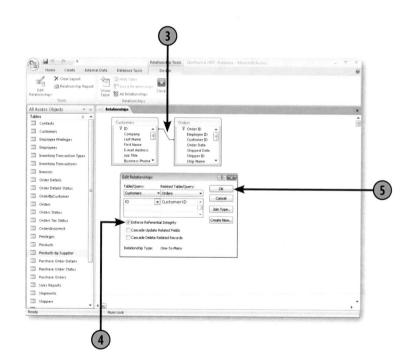

6

Customizing Fields

When you create a database table using a wizard, Microsoft Office Access 2007 assigns a data type and properties to each field in the table. When you create a table from scratch, or if you want to modify the settings Access applied to the table, you can change a field's properties so it stores data efficiently and interacts well with other fields in the database. Access 2007 also gives you several ways to facilitate accurate data entry. When you and your colleagues need to enter data such as phone numbers or postal codes, you can define an input mask that visually indicates the data pattern required for that field. If a field often contains the same value, you can set that value as the default. And, when there are only a few possible values for a field, such as when you need to select a category from your company's list of product categories, you can create a lookup list from which to choose the appropriate value or values. Finally, you can enable your colleagues to attach files, such as customer faxes, to a record, or create a memo field that enables users to add their own comments without being able to edit or delete existing comments.

Working with Tables

It's easy to create tables in Access, but you're not stuck with the first version of the table. After you create a table, you can modify it by adding, deleting, and reordering fields. While the order of your fields doesn't affect how your table functions within the database, changing the fields' order can make it easier for you and your colleagues to understand your table's structure when you view the table's data in Datasheet view and structure in Design view. In addition to the instructions to modify your table, this section includes a table that describes the data types available to you in Access 2007.

Delete a Field

① Open a table in Design view.

② Click the row selector of the row you want to delete.

③ Click the Delete Rows button.

④ Click Yes to confirm that you want to delete the row.

Caution

Deleting a primary key field prevents you from distinguishing a table row from other table rows or relating the table to other tables in your database.

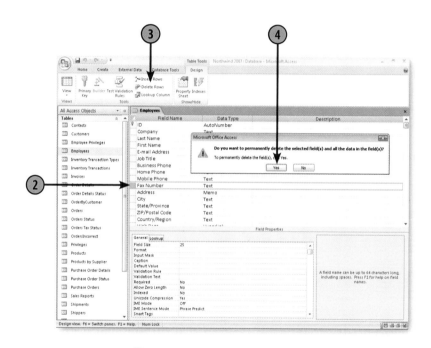

Tip

If you add a field to a table that already contains data, remember to set aside time to fill in the new data for any existing records.

Caution

Deleting a field gets rid of all the data in that field—it can't be retrieved. It's always a good idea to make a backup copy of a table when you make a significant change like deleting a field.

Add a Field

① Open a table in Design view.

② Click the row selector of the row below where you want the new field to appear.

③ Click the Insert Row button.

④ Type a name for the new field.

⑤ Assign a data type.

Arrange Fields

① Open a table in Design view.

② Click the row selector of the row you want to move.

③ Drag the row selector to the new position. A line appears to show where the row will be moved in the table.

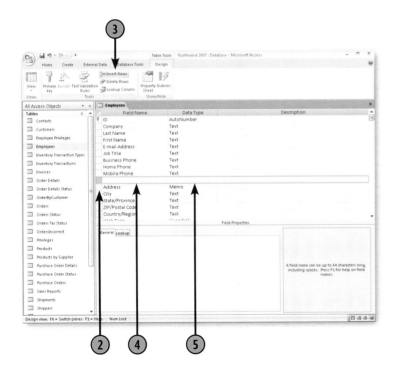

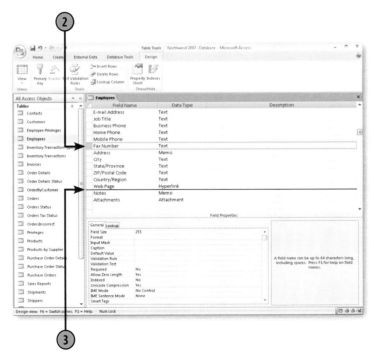

Assigning a Data Type

In Access, some operations such as arithmetic or date comparisons require you to assign the proper data type to a field. You have a number of data types to choose from, depending on your needs. For example, creating an AutoNumber field directs Access to add a sequential value to a table row automatically, which is useful for distinguishing a particular table row from all other rows in the table. Creating a memo field gives you and your colleagues a place to type notes about a table record, making it possible for information workers to add details as to why they entered data in a certain way, or to add customer comments.

Pick a Data Type

1. Open a table in Design view.
2. Click in the Data Type box of the field you want to edit.
3. Click the down arrow.
4. Click the data type to assign to the field.

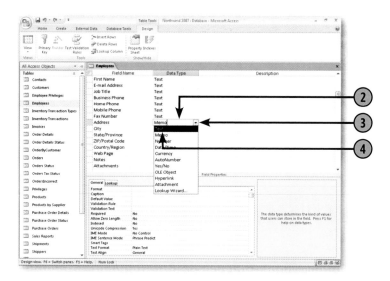

Available Data Types

Data Type	Description
Text	A series of numbers and letters of up to 255 characters
Memo	Same as the Text data type, with an upper limit of 64,000 characters
Number	Numeric data
Date/Time	Dates and times, between the years 100 and 9999
Currency	Primarily monetary amounts, but can also be used to set a specific number of digits to the right of the decimal point
AutoNumber	A unique number for each row, either one greater than the value in the most recently created row or a random value
Yes/No	A Yes/No, On/Off, or True/False value
OLE Object	A link to another file, such as a Microsoft Word document
Hyperlink	A link that opens a file, a location in a file, or a Web address
Lookup	A list of values derived from either an existing table (or query) field or from a list you enter directly; you can choose to allow users to assign multiple values to the field
Attachment	A file, or set of files, included as part of the record

Viewing or Changing Field Properties

Every field has a number of properties, such as the maximum number of characters allowed in the field. Setting a field's properties helps control the type of data entered into the field, which makes it less likely that your colleagues will enter erro-

neous data. The properties available to you are different for each data type, but you can view all of the available properties in the Field Properties pane, which appears at the bottom of the screen when you open a table in Design view.

View Field Properties

1. Open a table in Design view.

2. Click within the row representing the field with the properties you want to change.

3. Click the name of the property you want to change.

4. Follow any of these steps:

   ■ Type a new value for the property.

   ■ Click the down arrow, and choose a new value from the list.

   ■ Click the Build button to open the Expression Builder.

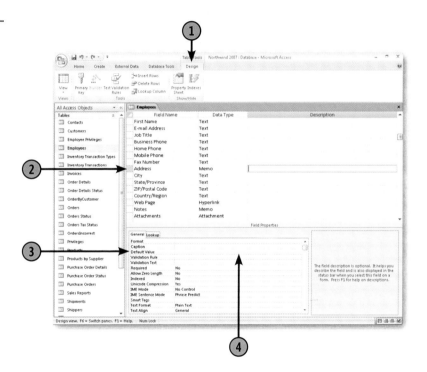

Introducing the Expression Builder

When you set a validation rule to check field data or when you create a calculation to find the total value of an order, you create an expression to evaluate the contents of one or more table fields. Rather than make you memorize how to identify the fields you want to use or which operators are available, you can use the controls in the Expression Builder to create your expressions quickly.

The expression appears here.

These buttons let you insert common functions, operators, and constants.

Click OK when you've created your expression.

Double-click to see a list of available functions.

Click Help to get more help on using the Expression Builder.

Click to see a list of available constants.

The available items for a group (or subgroup) appear here.

Click to see a list of available operators.

Click a subgroup to narrow the list of functions, constants, or operators displayed.

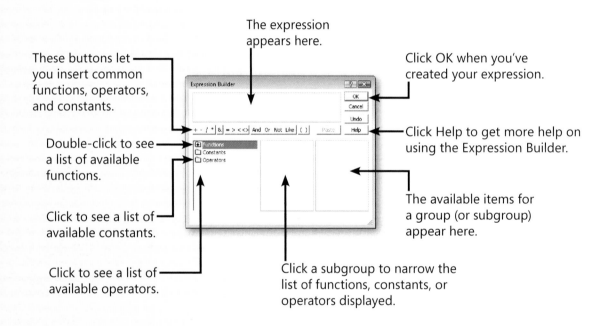

Formatting Field Contents

Access lets you choose how to display the contents of data in your tables. For example, you can display the field's contents in all uppercase or lowercase letters, change the color of the text, or display characters in addition to the data entered into the field. For example, if a product is only available by the case, adding the word "cases" after the number would remove any confusion as to the quantity being ordered. Adding formatting instructions only changes how data is displayed—it doesn't affect the data itself.

Change Field Format

① Open a table in Design view.

② Click the name of the field to format.

③ Type the formatting instructions in the Format property box.

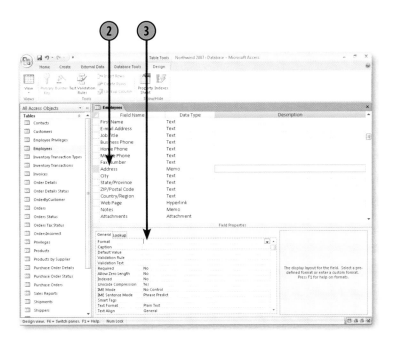

Tip

A down arrow appears in the Format property box when the box is active; clicking the down arrow displays a list of recently used formats. To reuse a format, simply click it.

Character	Resulting Format
!	Left align
<	Lowercase
>	Uppercase
&	Instruction to follow.
"Text"	Display the text as it appears between the quotes. &" kg" displays the value "16" as "16 kg."
(space)	Insert a blank space.
\	Display the next character as entered. **&\m** displays the text "100" as "100m."
@	Require a character; **@@@-@@@@** displays the text "5550011" as "555-0101."
*	Fill all blank spaces in the field with the named character. In a field with a maximum character property of eight, **&*#** displays "five" as "five####."
[color]	Display the field's contents in one of the eight available named colors (black, blue, green, cyan, red, magenta, yellow, and white).

Creating Input Masks

Databases are only as good as the data they hold, so it's important that you and your colleagues enter data correctly. You can guide data entry in text and date fields by creating an input mask, which gives you a template to follow when entering data in a field. For example, if your company's product codes follow a particular pattern, you can establish that pattern by using an input mask, ensuring that you and your colleagues enter the right sort of data into the field.

Define an Input Mask

1. Open a table in Design view.
2. Click the field for which you want to create the input mask.
3. Click in the Input Mask property box.
4. Click the Build button.
5. Click Yes to save the table.
6. Click the desired input mask.
7. Type values in the Try It box to ensure the input mask works as expected.
8. Click Next.

(continued on the next page)

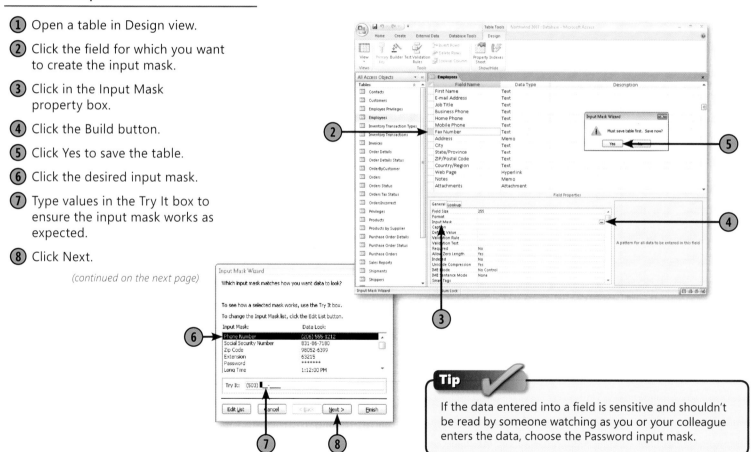

> **Tip**
>
> If the data entered into a field is sensitive and shouldn't be read by someone watching as you or your colleague enters the data, choose the Password input mask.

Define an Input Mask *(continued)*

9 To choose a new placeholder character, click the Place-holder down arrow, and then click the new character.

10 Click Next.

11 Select the option indicating whether you want to store the data as entered or with the characters in the input mask.

12 Click Finish.

Tip

Assign the Text data type to fields holding phone numbers so that you can take advantage of the Phone Number input mask.

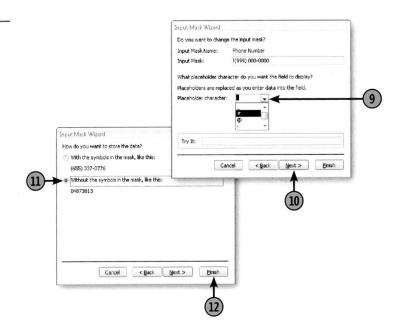

Edit an Input Mask

① Click the field to which you assigned an input mask.

② Click in the Input Mask property box.

③ Change the input mask using the available symbols.

Symbol	Description
0	Required digit (0 to 9)
9	Optional digit (0 to 9)
#	Any digit or space
L	Required letter
?	Optional letter
>	Makes following characters uppercase
<	Makes following characters lowercase
A	Required alphanumeric character
a	Optional alphanumeric character
&	Requires any character or space
C	Optional character or space

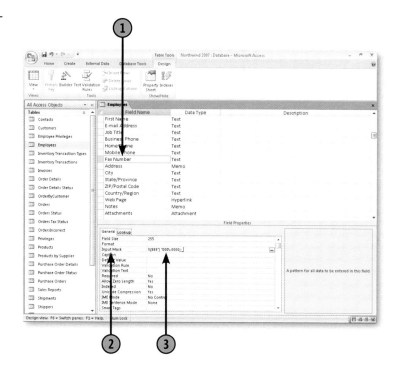

Tip

You can also reopen the Input Mask Wizard by clicking the Build button at the right edge of the Input Mask property box.

Assigning Required Fields and Requiring Data Entry

Some data is more important than other data. For example, a salesperson might need to know a contact's phone number, but not necessarily the contact's address. You can tell Access to prevent someone from moving beyond a required field without entering a value. For text and memo fields, you can require users to enter at least one character of text.

Require Data Entry

(1) Open a table in Design view.

(2) Click the field for which you want to require data entry.

(3) Click in the Required property box.

(4) Click the down arrow.

(5) Click Yes.

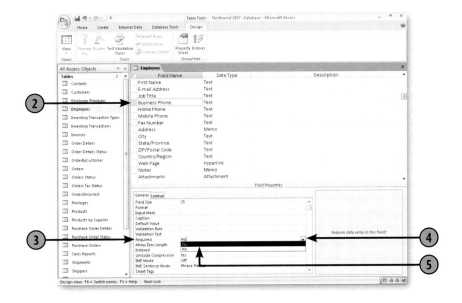

Disallow Zero-Length Strings

1. Open a table in Design view.
2. Click the text or memo field for which you want to require the user to enter at least one character of text.
3. Click in the Allow Zero Length property box.
4. Click the down arrow.
5. Click No.

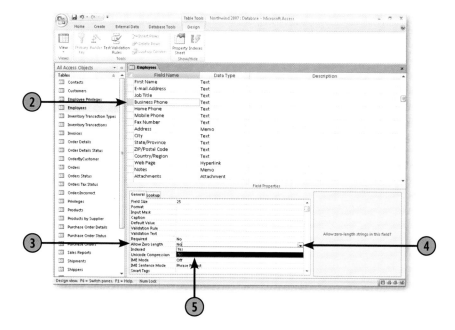

Setting Default Values

When you enter data, you often find that you enter the same value in a field many times. For example, most of your customers might come from the United States, but you have a Country field for those customers outside the United States. Setting a default value for a field saves you the trouble of entering the expected data over and over while still allowing you to edit the value if needed.

Assign a Default Value

① Open a table in Design view.

② Click the field to which you want to assign the default value.

③ Type the default value in the Default Value box.

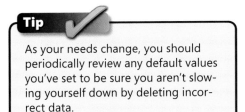

Tip

As your needs change, you should periodically review any default values you've set to be sure you aren't slowing yourself down by deleting incorrect data.

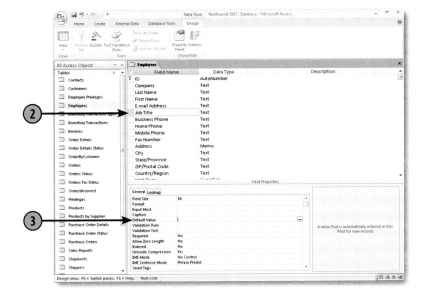

Indexing Field Values

When you create an index of a field's values, Access maintains an internal record of the values in a field, which the program can then use to find table records with specific values. Access always keeps an index of a table's primary key field's values.

Create an Index

① Open a table in Design view.

② Click the field to index.

③ Click the Indexed property name.

④ Click the Indexed down arrow.

⑤ Click either Yes (Duplicates OK) or Yes (No Duplicates).

Try This!

Open the Northwind sample database, click Tables on the Objects bar, double-click Products, and then click Design. Click any cell in the ProductName row of the design grid, and then click Indexed in the Field Properties section. Click the down arrow that appears, and then click Yes (No Duplicates). This change requires every new product entered into the table to have a unique name. This specific change works for Northwind, which carries unique products, but may not work for a business that buys common items from more than one supplier.

Tip

Indexes work best in fields with lots of different values. In large tables, indexing the values in commonly used fields lets Access find what you're looking for quickly.

Caution

Access updates all of its indexes every time you add or update a table record. Creating unneeded indexes can greatly slow down data entry, especially on older systems.

Validating Data Entry

Some categories of data, such as credit limits or the date someone joined a club, have to meet certain criteria. You can make sure data entered into fields meets those criteria (for example, all credit limits are $5,000 or less) by performing data validation. When a user tries to enter data that isn't appropriate for the field, you can display a message letting the user know what went wrong.

Perform Data Validation

1. Open a table in Design view.
2. Click the field for which you want to validate data entry.
3. Click Validation Rule.
4. Click the Build button.
5. Create the validation rule in the Expression Builder.
6. Click OK.

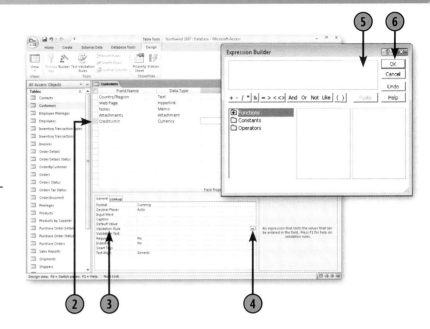

Set Validation Text

1. Open a table in Design view.
2. Click the field to which you want to assign validation text.
3. Type your validation text in the Validation Text box.

 **Tip**

You can type your validation rule, such as **<=5000**, directly into the Validation Rule box.

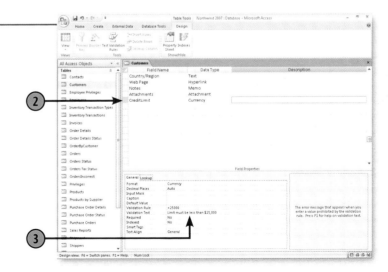

Creating a Lookup Field

Many times the data you need to enter in one table can be found in another table. In the Northwind database, for example, if you add a new product, you must assign it to a category. Rather than make you open the Categories table separately and find the value you need, Access lets you display those values in a list. You can also create your own list, rather than drawing values from an existing source.

Define a Field as a Lookup Field

1. Open a table in Design view.

2. Click the field to define as a lookup field.

3. Click the Data Type cell, click the down arrow, and then click Lookup Wizard.

4. Select the I Want the Lookup Column to Look Up the Values in a Table or Query option.

5. Click Next.

6. Click the table or query to provide the values.

7. Click Next.

(continued on the next page)

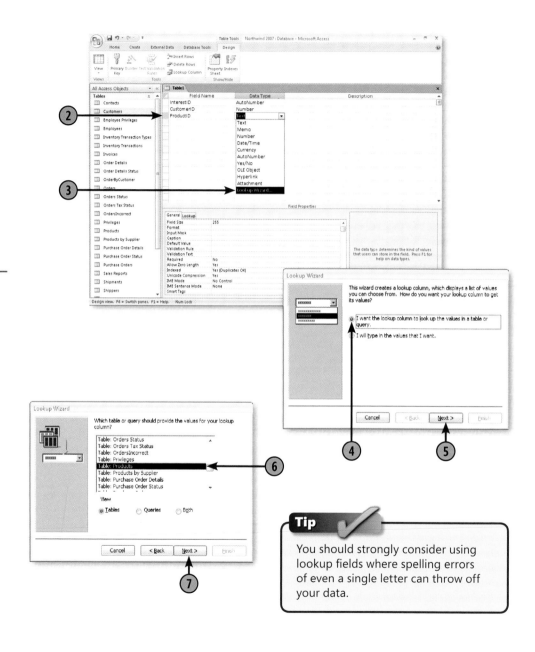

Tip

You should strongly consider using lookup fields where spelling errors of even a single letter can throw off your data.

Define a Field as a Lookup Field *(continued)*

⑧ Click the first field to provide the values.

⑨ Click the Add button.

⑩ Repeat steps 6 and 7 to add more fields.

⑪ Click Next.

⑫ Click the first sorting field's down arrow.

⑬ Click the name of the field by which you want to sort the values of the lookup column.

⑭ Click the sorting order button to toggle between Ascending and Descending order.

⑮ Click Next.

⑯ Click Finish.

Tip

Leave the Hide key column check box selected so the person using the lookup column only sees the values in the field you want him or her to see, not the values in the primary key field.

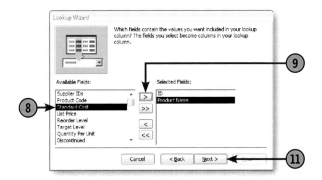

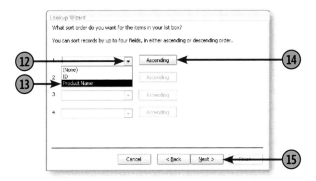

Allow Multiple Selections from a Lookup Field

① Open a table in Design view.

② Click the field to define as a lookup field.

③ Click the Data Type cell, click the down arrow, and then click Lookup Wizard.

④ Select the I Want the Lookup Column to Look Up the Values in a Table or Query option.

⑤ Click Next.

⑥ Click the table or query to provide the values.

⑦ Click Next.

⑧ Click the first field to provide the values.

⑨ Click Add.

⑩ Click Next three times.

⑪ Select the Allow Multiple Values check box.

⑫ Click Finish.

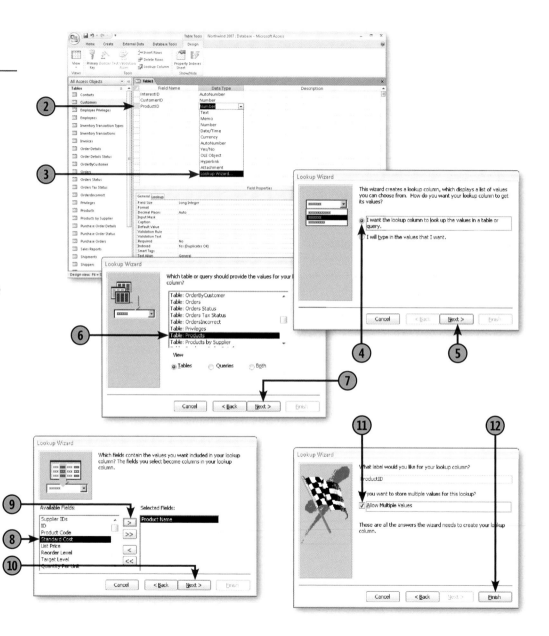

Draw Lookup Values from a Data List

① Open a table in Design view.

② Click the field to define as a lookup field.

③ Click the Data Type cell, click the down arrow, and then click Lookup Wizard.

④ Select the I Will Type In The Values That I Want option.

⑤ Click Next.

⑥ Type the number of columns you want in your lookup list.

⑦ Type the first row of values in the list, and then press Tab.

⑧ Continue adding rows until all values are in the list.

⑨ Click Finish.

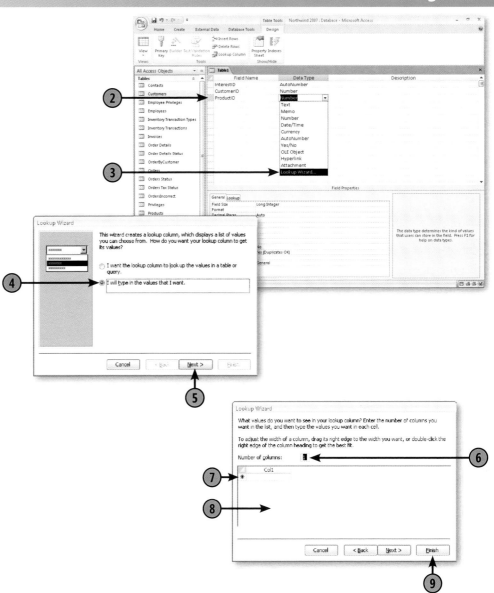

Creating an Append-Only Memo Field

Most database table fields contain dry, factual data such as prices, quantities, and descriptions. You can extend the facts in your tables by creating memo fields, which can contain up to 64,000 characters. Memo fields are ideal for storing comments about database records, but you might not want to allow users to delete existing comments. To allow users to add but not delete comments to a memo field, you can make the memo field an append-only field.

Create an Append-Only Field

① Open a table in Design view.

② Click the field to define as an append-only field.

③ Click the Data Type cell.

④ Click the down arrow.

⑤ Click Memo.

⑥ Click the Append Only property.

⑦ Click the down arrow.

⑧ Click Yes.

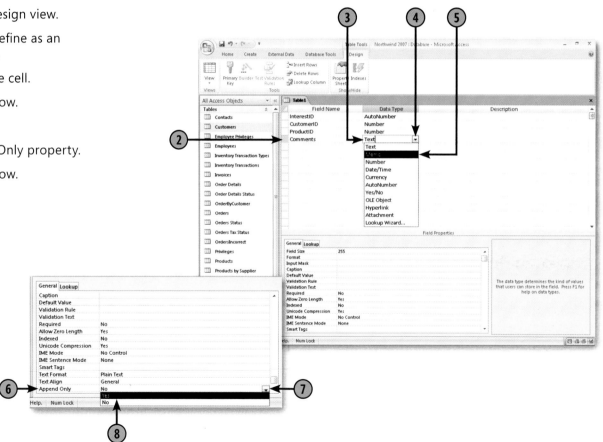

Creating an Attachment Field

Databases can contain information about business transactions, but there's a lot more to business than simple numerical and text values. If you work with paper invoices, purchase orders, or correspondence, you can scan those documents into electronic form and attach the documents to the record

to which the documents are related. Alternatively, if you have another file (such as a Word document, product image, or Excel workbook) that's related to the item described by the record, you can also attach those files to the record.

Create an Attachment Field

① Open a table in Design view.

② Click the field to define as an attachment field.

③ Click the Data Type cell.

④ Click the down arrow.

⑤ Click Attachment.

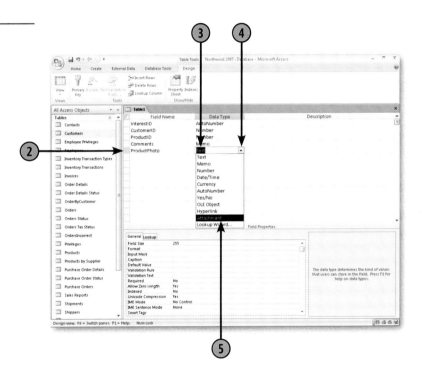

7

Customizing Tables

In section 6, I explained how to change a table's structure by working with the table in Design view. This section shows you how to work with a table in Datasheet view, in which the table data is displayed in a datasheet where each column represents a table field and each row represents a table record. Changing how your data is displayed in Datasheet view can make your table easier to read and work with—for example, you might change the order of fields in a table to reflect the natural order you and your colleagues follow when entering data from a paper form into the table. In this section, you will learn how to manipulate table columns and rows, find and replace text, enter data using AutoCorrect, view a subdatasheet, and filter table records.

Finding and Replacing Text

After you enter data into a table, you might need to search the table for a particular word, or if one of your suppliers changes the name of a product, you might need to replace some or all instances of a word or phrase. You can do that using the Find and Replace tools in Microsoft Office Access 2007. But be careful when you replace text! If you replace every occurrence of the word *chip* with the word *crisp*, you could end up selling *chocolate crisp cookies*.

Find Text

(1) Open a table in Datasheet view.

(2) Click the Home tab.

(3) Click Find.

(4) Type the text you want to find in the Find What field.

(5) Click the Look In down arrow, and click the field or table where you expect to find the text.

(6) Click the Match down arrow, and then choose one of these options:

- Click Whole Field to return table records where your text matches the entire contents of a field.

- Click Any Part Of Field to return table records where your text is found within a field.

- Click Start Of Field to return table records where your text is found at the beginning of a field.

(7) Click Find Next.

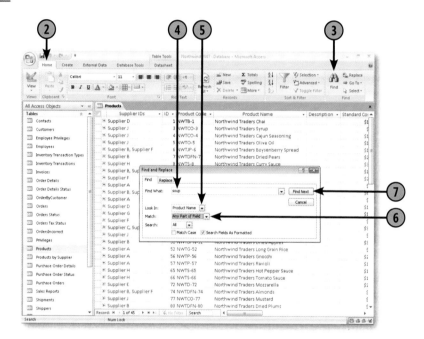

Replace Text

① Open a table in Datasheet view.

② Click the Home tab.

③ Click Replace.

④ Type the text you want to replace in the Find What box.

⑤ Type the text to substitute for the original text in the Replace With box.

⑥ Click the Look In down arrow, and click the field or table where you expect to find the text.

⑦ Click the Match down arrow, and then choose one of these options:

- ■ Click Whole Field to return table records where your text matches the entire contents of a field.

- ■ Click Any Part Of Field to return table records where your text is found within a field.

- ■ Click Start Of Field to return table records where your text is found at the beginning of a field.

⑧ Click Find Next to locate the first instance of the text to be replaced.

⑨ Click Replace.

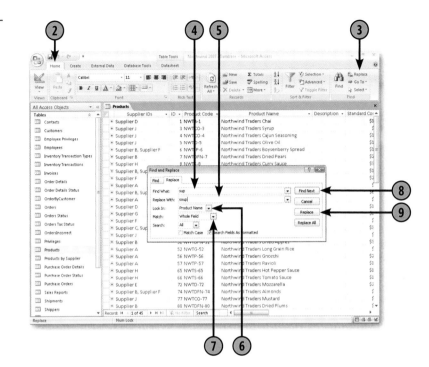

Entering Data Using AutoCorrect

When you enter data into a table, Access examines what you type and corrects any common spelling errors it knows about. You can also add your own AutoCorrect values to streamline data entry—for example, you could have Access recognize the abbreviation *sarsp* and replace it with *sarsaparilla*. If you find that Access insists on changing a text entry that you know is correct, you can delete a particular AutoCorrect entry. As an example, one of your projects might have the code name AMDE, which Access automatically changes to MADE.

Add Text with AutoCorrect

1 Open a table in Datasheet view.

2 Begin typing text in a cell.

3 When a value AutoCorrect recognizes appears, the program replaces the incorrect value with the correct value.

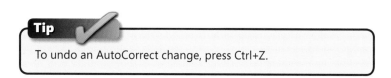

Tip

To undo an AutoCorrect change, press Ctrl+Z.

Turn AutoCorrect On or Off

(1) Click the Microsoft Office button.

(2) Click Access Options.

(3) Click Proofing.

(4) Click AutoCorrect Options.

(5) Do either of the following:

■ Select the Replace Text As You Type check box to turn on AutoCorrect.

■ Deselect the Replace Text As You Type check box to turn off AutoCorrect.

(6) Click OK.

(7) Click OK.

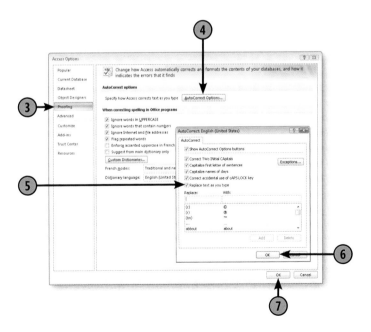

Tip

If you want to have Access *not* correct a particular entry, click the AutoCorrect Options smart tag that appears when it makes a correction. From the menu that appears, click Stop Automatically Correcting *"entry"*. Clicking Change Back to *"entry"* from the AutoCorrect Options smart tag's list undoes this change without deleting the rule.

Add AutoCorrect Values

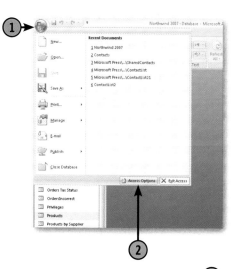

① Click the Microsoft Office button.

② Click Access Options.

③ Click Proofing.

④ Click AutoCorrect Options.

⑤ Type the text to be replaced in the Replace box.

⑥ Type the text to substitute for the entered text in the With box.

⑦ Click Replace.

⑧ Click OK.

⑨ Click OK.

Try This!

Click the Office button and then click Access Options. Click Proofing and then type *sarsp* in the Replace box, type *sarsaparilla* in the With box, and click Add. Click OK to close the Auto-Correct dialog box. Now every time you type *sarsp*, AutoCorrect replaces it with *sarsaparilla*.

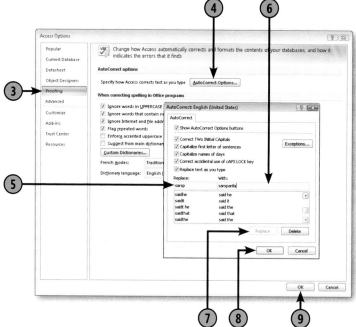

Adding and Editing Text

Once you open a table, you can edit the existing data, add new data, or copy data from one cell and paste it into another. You can edit text using the same techniques that you use in other Microsoft Office 2007 applications. When you cut or copy table data, the Office Clipboard keeps track of the last 24 items you cut or copy. If you want Access to undo the last change you made, you can do so by pressing Ctrl+Z or by clicking the Undo button on the Quick Access Toolbar.

Select Text

- Move the mouse pointer over a cell until the pointer turns into a white cross, and then click in the cell.

- Double-click a word to select it.

- Drag the mouse pointer over text to select it.

Delete Text

- Click to the right of the text to be deleted, and press Backspace to delete it one character at a time.

- Select the text and press Delete.

Undoing Operations

- To undo an operation, click the Undo button in the Quick Access Toolbar.

Move the mouse ...

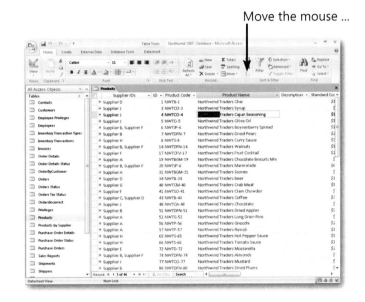

Copy and Paste Text

① Select the text you want to copy.

② Click the Home tab.

③ Click the Copy button.

④ Click the position where you want to paste the text.

⑤ Click the Paste button.

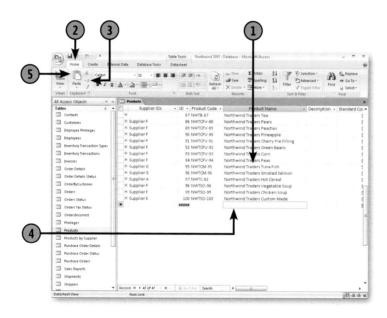

Copy and Paste Items with the Office Clipboard

(1) On the Home tab, click the Clipboard group's dialog box launcher.

(2) Select the contents of a cell and click Copy.

(3) Click the cell where you want to paste the contents.

(4) Click the item to be pasted.

(5) Click the down arrow.

(6) Click Paste.

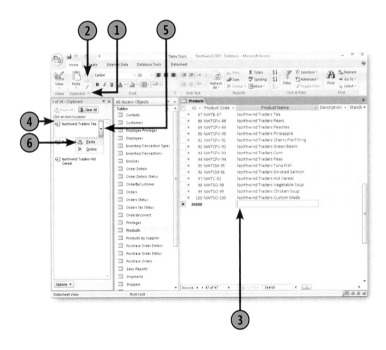

Manipulating Columns

You can change how data is displayed in your datasheet by changing the order of the table's columns. You can also add or delete fields by inserting a column (which creates a new field) or deleting a column (which deletes the field it represents). If you want to copy the contents of a column to another table, or even to another Office document, you can do so easily.

Relocate a Column

① Click the column head of the column you want to move.

② Drag the column to its new position in the datasheet. A vertical black line appears on the edge between the two columns where the moved column will be pasted.

Caution

Be sure to release the mouse button after you click the column head; if you don't, you'll select more than one column instead of moving only the column you want to move.

Insert a Column

① Right-click the column head of the column to the right of where you want the new column to appear.

② Choose Insert Column from the shortcut menu.

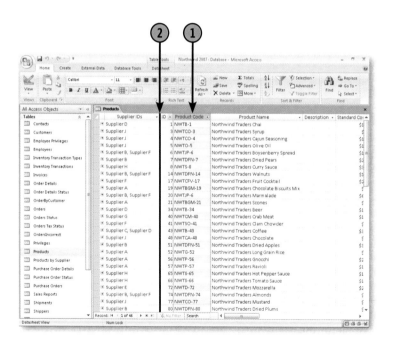

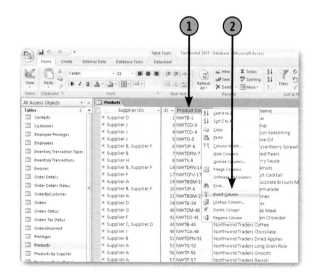

Rename a Column

① Right-click the column head of the column.

② Choose Rename Column from the shortcut menu.

③ Type a new name for the column and press Enter.

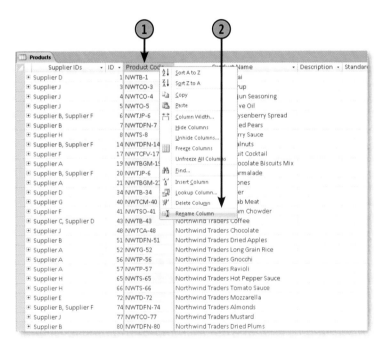

Copy a Column

① Right-click the column head of the column you want to copy.

② Choose Copy from the shortcut menu.

③ Click the column head of a blank column.

④ Click the Paste button.

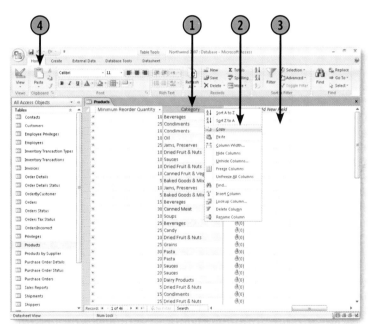

Modifying Columns and Rows

The standard height of datasheet rows is just enough to display the contents of a row. While that setting fits a lot of data on a sheet, it doesn't always make it easy to read the row's contents. You can increase the height of your table's rows or change the width of individual columns to show more or less of the row or column's contents. Bear in mind that you can't change the height of individual rows; changes you make to one row affect every row in your table.

> **Tip**
>
> To change the width of more than one column, select the columns to change, move the mouse pointer over the edge of any of those columns' selectors, and drag the edge to the desired width. Every selected column takes on the new setting.

Change Row Height

① Move the mouse pointer over an edge of a row selector.

② Drag the edge up or down.

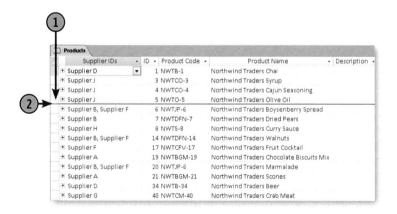

Change Column Width

① Move the mouse pointer over an edge of the column selector of the column you want to resize.

② Drag the edge to the left or right.

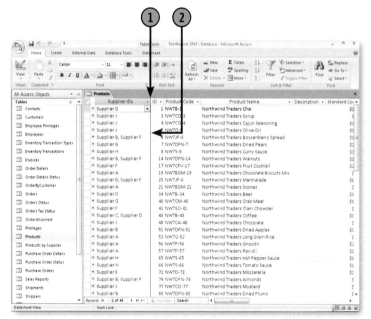

Viewing a Subdatasheet

When two tables are in a one-to-many relationship, you can create a subdatasheet that displays records from the table on the "many" side of the relationship. A plus sign appears next to the key field of the datasheet on the "one" side of the rela-tionship, indicating a subdatasheet is available. If your table doesn't have a subdatasheet associated with it, you can set your table's properties to identify the table or query that you want to display as a subdatasheet.

Open and Close a Subdatasheet

1. Open a table in Datasheet view.

2. Click the plus sign next to the value for which you want to see records in the related subdatasheet.

3. Click the minus sign to hide the subdatasheet.

> **See Also**
>
> For more information about relationships, see "Creating Relationships between Tables" on page 46.

Create a Subdatasheet

1. Open a table in Design view.

2. Click the Design tab.

3. Click Property Sheet.

4. Click the Subdatasheet Name property field, click the down arrow that appears, and then click the table or query to provide data for the subdatasheet.

5. If necessary, click the Link Child Fields down arrow, and then click the name of the foreign key field in the table to provide data for the subdatasheet.

6. Click the Close button to close the Property Sheet task pane.

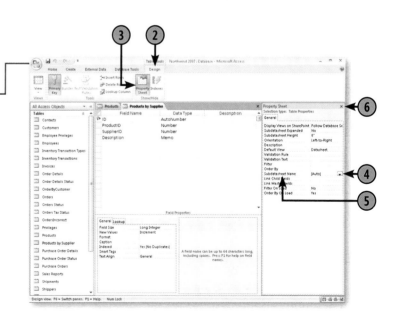

Filtering Table Records

Often you will be interested in viewing only some of the records in a table. For example, you might want to find all of your customers or suppliers from a particular state or country. You can narrow the records shown in a table by creating a filter, which hides records not meeting your criteria. The records aren't erased, though; when you remove the filter, they display normally.

Filter Table Records

1. Open a table in Datasheet view.
2. Select the text to serve as the base for the filter.
3. Click the Home tab.
4. Click Selection.
5. Click the type of filter you want to create.

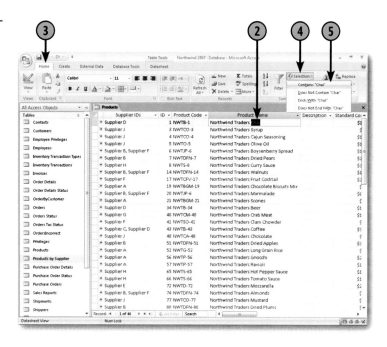

Filter by Form

1. Open a table in Datasheet view.
2. Click the Home tab.
3. Click Advanced.
4. Click Filter By Form.
5. Click the cell in the column by which you want to filter.
6. Click the down arrow that appears.
7. Select the value by which you want to filter.
8. Click the Toggle Filter button to apply the filter.

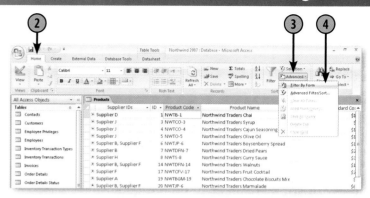

Remove a Filter

1. Click the Home tab.
2. Click Toggle Filter.

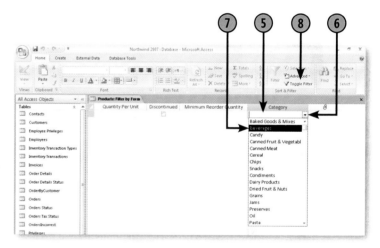

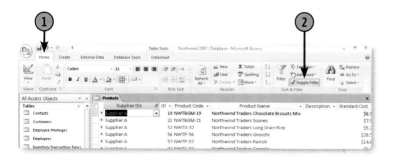

Filter Records by the Contents of More than One Column

1. Open a table in Datasheet view.
2. Click the Home tab.
3. Click Advanced.
4. Click Advanced Filter/Sort.
5. Click the down arrow in the first Field cell and then click the name of the field by which you want to filter.
6. Type the expression by which you want to filter the table.
7. Repeat steps 5 and 6 as needed to add other fields to the filter.
8. Click Toggle Filter.

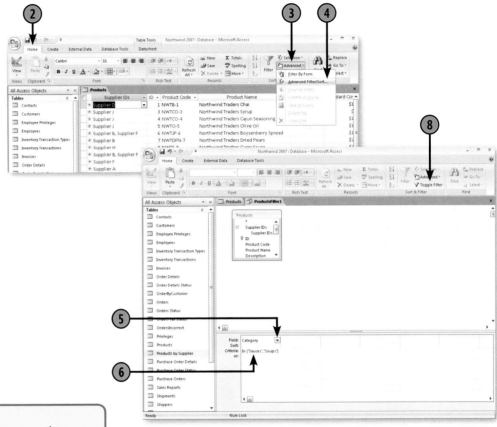

Try This!

Open the Northwind sample database and then open the Products table in Datasheet view. Click the Home tab, click Advanced, and then click Advanced Filter/Sort. Click in the first Field cell, click the down arrow that appears, and then click Category. In the Criteria cell of the first column, type **Beverages**. Click in the second column's Field cell, click the down arrow, and then click Standard Cost. Type **>10** in the second column's Criteria cell. In the Sort & Filter group on the ribbon, click Toggle Filter to display the filtered table. Click the Toggle Filter button again to remove the filter.

Tip

You can use the Expression Builder to create your filter by right-clicking in a Criteria cell and choosing the Build command from the submenu that appears.

Creating Forms

One of the nice things about Microsoft Office Access 2007 is that it makes it easy for you to view existing table data and even add new data using forms. A form is a database object that lets you enter and view table data without viewing the table in datasheet mode. Instead, you can create a form that spaces the data out on the page, limit the number of table fields displayed so that only the most important or relevant data is shown, and modify the form once you've created it to make the form easier to use.

Creating a Simple Form

Access makes it possible for you to create powerful and complex forms, but there will be plenty of occasions where a simple form that contains all of the fields from a table will meet your needs. Creating a simple form is a straightforward process: You select the table from which you want to create your form, tell Access you want to create a simple form based on that table, and you're done. The whole process takes a maximum of four mouse clicks from start to finish.

Create a Simple Form

① In the Navigation pane, click a table.

② Click the Create tab.

③ Click Form.

Creating a Form Using the Form Wizard

Access makes it easy for you to create forms based on the tables in your database. By using the Form Wizard, you can choose the data source, the type of the form, and the form's appearance. The Access 2007 version of the Form Wizard also includes a wide variety of form themes from which to choose, enabling you to create great-looking forms without doing any design work yourself.

Step through the Form Wizard

① Click the Create tab.

② Click More Forms.

③ Click Form Wizard.

(continued on the next page)

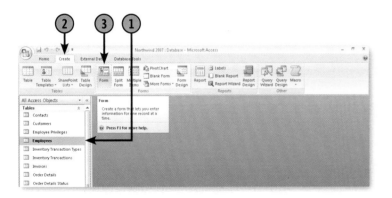

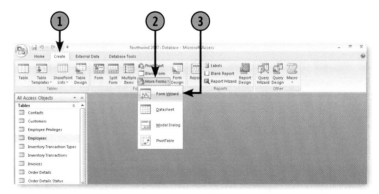

Step through the
Form Wizard *(continued)*

④ Click the Tables/Queries
down arrow.

⑤ Click the table to provide the
values and structure for the form.

⑥ Click a field in the Available
Fields box and then click either
of the following:

- Click Add to add the
selected field.

- Click Add All to add all fields to
the form.

⑦ Click Next.

⑧ Select the layout for the form.

⑨ Click Next.

⑩ Click the name of the style for
the form.

⑪ Click Next.

⑫ Type a name for
the form.

⑬ Click Finish.

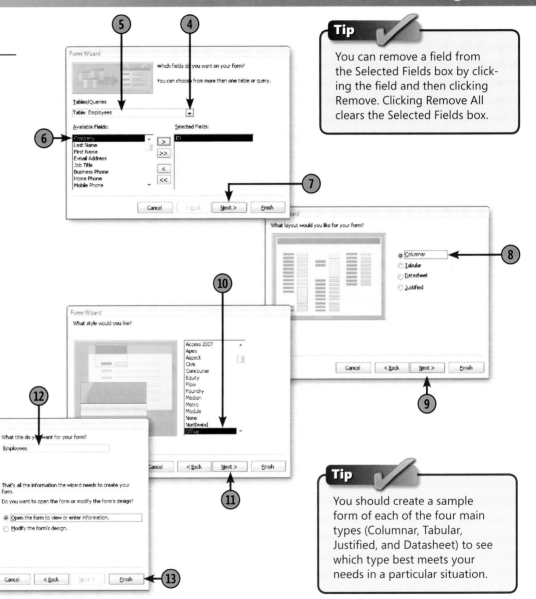

Tip ✓
You can remove a field from
the Selected Fields box by clicking the field and then clicking
Remove. Clicking Remove All
clears the Selected Fields box.

Tip ✓
You should create a sample
form of each of the four main
types (Columnar, Tabular,
Justified, and Datasheet) to see
which type best meets your
needs in a particular situation.

Creating a Form in Design View

If you'd rather not use the Form Wizard to create a form, you can open a blank form and manually add controls. If you want to add fields from a table to your form, you can display fields from existing tables by displaying the Add Existing Fields pane and dragging the desired fields to the body of the form.

Create a Form in Design View

1. Click the Create tab.
2. Click Form Design.
3. If necessary, click the Design contextual tab.
4. If necessary, click Property Sheet.
5. Click Data.
6. Click Record Source.
7. Click the down arrow.
8. Click the table from which you want to draw your values.

(continued on the next page)

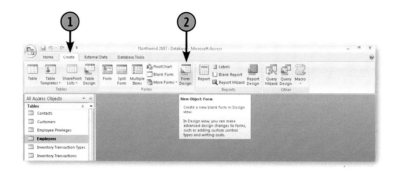

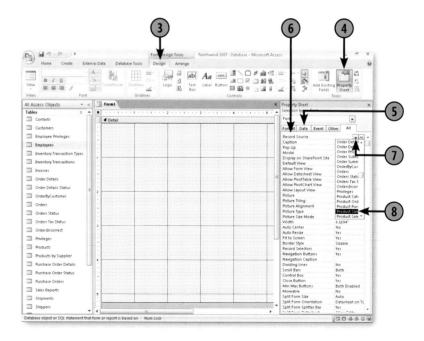

Create a Form in Design View *(continued)*

⑨ Click Add Existing Fields.

⑩ Drag fields from the Field List task pane to the body of the form.

⑪ Click Save.

⑫ Type a name for the form.

⑬ Click OK.

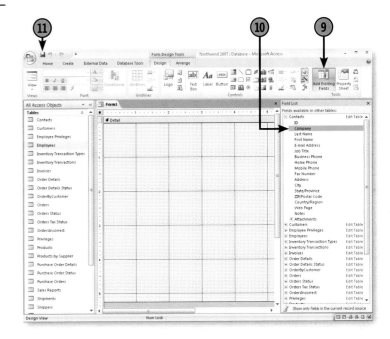

Caution

If the Property Sheet task pane is currently displayed, clicking the Property Sheet ribbon button will hide it.

Try This!

Open the Northwind sample database, display the Navigation Pane, and then click the Products table. On the Create tab, in the Forms group, click Form Design. After the form appears, on the Design contextual tab, in the Tools group, click Property Sheet. In the Property Sheet task pane, click the Record Source property name, click the down arrow that appears, and then click Products. On the Design contextual tab, in the Tools group, click Add Existing Fields. Drag the ID and Product Name fields to the body of the form. Click the Save button on the Quick Access Toolbar, type **ProductSample** in the dialog box that appears, and then click OK.

Creating a Multiple Items Form

In general, you use forms for data entry and for viewing table or query records. For those tasks, many users prefer to view one record at a time. Typing a new record into an otherwise blank form limits the distractions caused by other data. The same can be said of viewing a table or query; if you want to see more than one record at a time, you could view the table or query in Datasheet view.

The problem with Datasheet view is that it presents a basic grid that, though it has gridlines, doesn't make it very easy to distinguish one record from another. If you want to present or enter your data while still viewing other records in the table or query, you can create a Multiple Items Form. This type of form displays your data in a grid layout, but you have much more control over the grid and the data's appearance.

Create a Multiple Items Form

① Click the table or query from which you want to create the form.

② Click the Create tab.

③ Click Multiple Items.

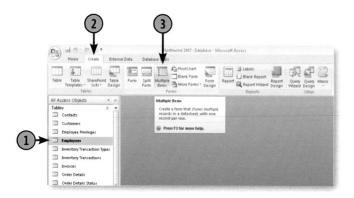

Modifying an Existing Form

Just as you can create a form from scratch, you can open a form in Design view to add or delete controls, change a form's appearance, or add and delete fields. Form controls, such as check boxes, text boxes, and labels, enable you to provide instructions for your colleagues and allow them to enter data as efficiently as possible. For example, if a field has two possible choices, such as *true* and *false*, you can create a check box that reflects those values by being either checked or unchecked.

Open a Form for Editing in Design View

① Display the forms in your database in the Navigation pane.

② Right-click a form.

③ Click Design View.

See Also

For more information about modifying forms, see "Beautifying Forms and Reports" on page 143.

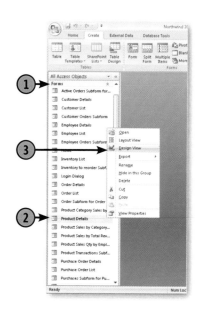

Display the Field List

① Display a form in Design view.

② Click the Design contextual tab.

③ If necessary, click Add Existing Fields.

Hide the Field List

■ Click the Close box to hide the Field List task pane.

Add a Field to a Form

① Drag the field from the Field List task pane to the desired spot on the form.

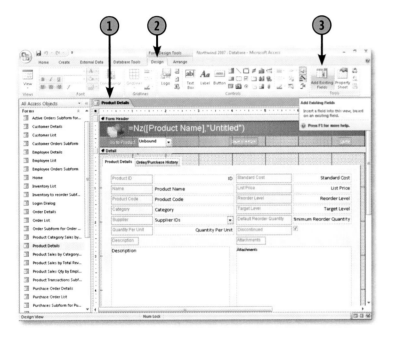

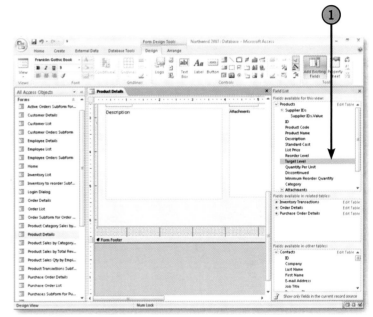

Adding and Deleting Form Controls

After you open a form in Design view, you can add or remove text boxes, option buttons, and images from the form. You can also modify a control's properties to change the control's appearance or to define where the control gets its data. Deleting unnecessary fields makes more room for the remaining fields and helps to control unwanted data entry. For example, if you find that your tables contain a field that some of your co-workers aren't supposed to fill in, such as a customer's credit limit, you can create a form that includes every table field and then delete the credit limit field.

Add a Control with a Wizard

1. Open a form in Design view.

2. If necessary, click the Design contextual tab.

3. If necessary, click the Use Control Wizards button.

4. On the ribbon, click the control you want to add.

5. Drag the mouse pointer on the form to define the control's area.

6. Follow the steps in the wizard (if applicable) to define the contents of the control.

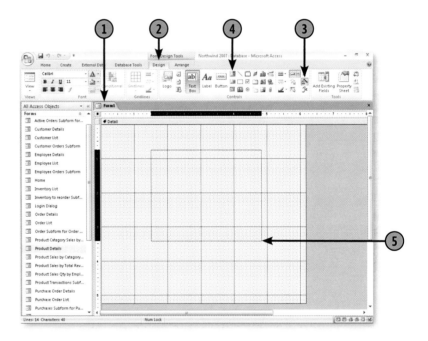

Delete a Control

1. Display a form in Design view.

2. Right-click the control.

3. Choose Delete from the shortcut menu.

Tip

Be sure to click the control itself, not the label next to the control.

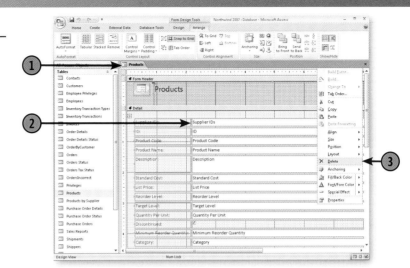

Modify Control Properties

1. Display a form in Design view.

2. Click the control.

3. Click the Design contextual tab.

4. Click Property Sheet.

5. Click the property to change.

6. Follow any of these steps:

   ◼ Type a new value in the text box next to the property name.

   ◼ Click the down arrow, and select a new property from the list that appears.

   ◼ Click the Build button, and use the dialog box that appears to select or construct a new value.

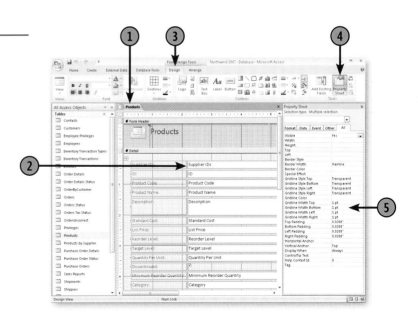

Available Control Types

Control	Description
Label	Text that is not tied to a field or other control.
Text box	A control that holds the contents of an existing table or query field or that has been typed by a user.
Toggle button	A button that can either be on or off, representing an independent value of on/off, true/false, or yes/no.
Option button	An independent option that represents an independent value. When grouped, only one option button may be selected at a time.
Check box	An independent option that can be selected or cleared. When two or more check boxes are included in the same Option Group control (mentioned elsewhere in this table), only one check box may be selected.
List box	A control that allows a user to pick a value from a list entered by the form's creator or that is derived from a table or query.
Combo box	A control that allows a user to enter a value or pick a value from a list entered by the form's creator or that is derived from a table or query.
Command button	A button that, when clicked, executes a macro or other set of instructions linked to the button.
Image	A control that holds an image or graphic.
Unbound object frame	A control that holds a linked file.
Bound object frame	A control that holds an embedded file.
Page break	A control that separates a form into two (or more) printed pages.
Tab page	A control with multiple pages, accessed by folder tabs at the top of the control.
Subform/Subreport	A form or report that displays records from a form or report on the "many" side of a one-to-many relationship.
Line	A control that lets you draw a line on a form.
Rectangle	A control that lets you draw a rectangle.
Option Group	An outline you place around a group of controls such as check boxes or option buttons. Only one control in the group may be selected at a time.

Adding a Date Picker Control

It seems like using dates in Access and, for that matter, every other program should be simple, but that's not always the case. Many Web applications, such as flight reservation systems, require you to enter dates using a date picker control that displays a month at a time. You can scroll from month to month and make your choice by clicking the day you want to leave when you display the right month.

You can add a similar control to your Access forms by creating a date picker control. This control, which is based on the date picker controls found in Microsoft Office Outlook 2007, enables users to decide on the date they want without you having to worry if 2/12/2007 means February 12, 2007 (as in the United States), or December 2, 2007 (as in many European countries).

Add a Date Picker

1. Open a form in Design view.
2. Click a form control that is bound to a field that contains dates.
3. If necessary, click the Design tab.
4. If necessary, click Property Sheet.
5. Click Format.
6. Click Show Date Picker.
7. Click the down arrow that appears.
8. Click For Dates.

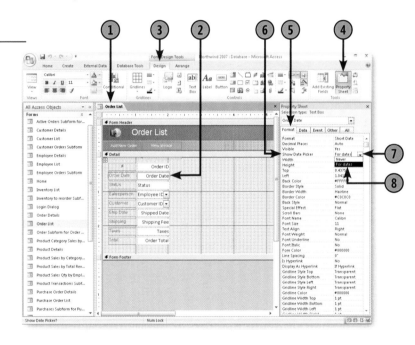

Tip

If you don't want Access to display a date picker for the selected field, set the Show Date Picker property's value to *Never*.

Creating a Subform

When you create a form that shows the records from a table on the "one" side of a one-to-many relationship, you can create a subform to display records from the table on the "many" side of the relationship. You can also change how the subform displays its records. If you want to see the records as a datasheet, you can change the subform's view so that it displays the related records while making best use of the form's space.

Add a Subform

① Open a form based on a table on the "one" side of a one-to-many relationship in Design view.

② Click the Design contextual tab.

③ Click the Subform/Subreport control.

④ On the form, drag to define the area where the subform should appear.

⑤ Select the Use An Existing Form option.

⑥ Click the form to supply the data for the subform.

⑦ Click Next.

(continued on the next page)

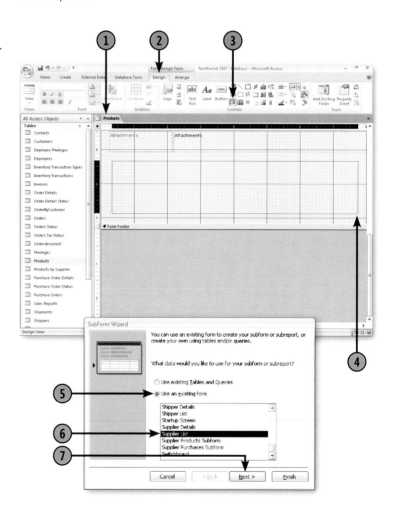

Tip

You can get help on using subforms and subreports by going to the last page of the Subform Wizard and selecting the Display Help On Using Subforms or Subreports check box and clicking Finish.

See Also

For more information about relationships, see "Creating Relationships between Tables" on page 46.

Creating a Subform *(continued)*

⑧ Click Next to have the wizard draw the values from the form you selected.

⑨ Type Subform after the end of the form name.

⑩ Click Finish.

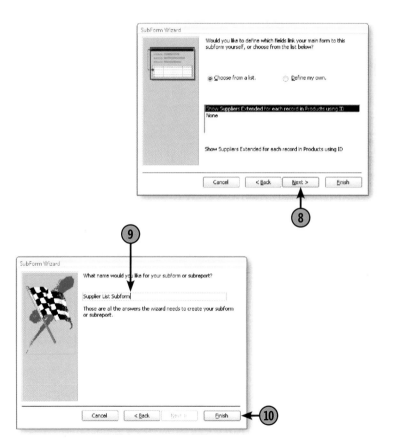

Change Subform Views

① Display the form that contains the subform in Form view.

② Right-click any spot on the body of the subform.

③ Click the desired view from the shortcut menu.

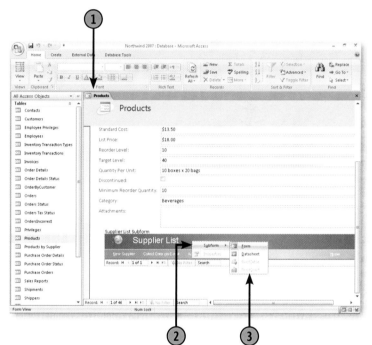

Tip ✓

To change the subform from Datasheet view back to Form view, click the Design View button and then click the Form View button.

Displaying a Form and Its Datasheet Simultaneously

Subforms enable you to display the data from two related tables or queries in a single form. What they don't enable you to do, however, is display the entire datasheet from which the form draws its data. If you create a subform that displays the same data as the main form, it only displays the current record, not the entire datasheet.

Create a Split Form

① Click the table to serve as the source of your form data.

② Click the Create tab.

③ Click Split Form.

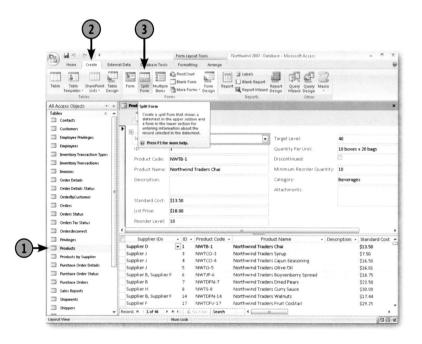

Creating Queries

The database object used to store data is the table, but even the best-designed table has limitations. For example, if a table holds more than a few dozen records, it's difficult to look through the table and find records that meet a particular criterion. You may want to display all orders from a specific customer without having to wade through the entire table to find them.

Enter the query. A query is an Access object that lets you find just those table records you're interested in, whether you want to see all orders from customers in Germany or to identify customers who have never placed an order. You can also create queries that let you and your colleagues type the value for which they want to search; rather than always search for orders by customers in Germany, you could create a query that asks which country to look for.

Introducing Query Types

When you want to retrieve table records that meet particular criteria, you create a query. The type of query you create, however, depends on the records you want to return and what, if anything, you want Access to do with the results.

The most basic query type is the *select query*, which reaches into one or more database tables and locates records. While you can have Access return every field in a record, you can also choose which fields are displayed in the results. For example, you could get information about customers that placed an order in a given month and, instead of displaying every field relating to the company, just display the company's name. You can also limit the records returned by the query by specifying one or more criteria or rules the query uses when

deciding which table rows to return. Should your table contain data that relates to two different values, such as a company name and sales representatives, you can create a crosstab query to display the quantity of items sold by each employee to each company (as shown below).

A version of the select query is the *parameter query*. Like a select query, the parameter query uses one or more criteria to limit the records returned by the query. The difference, however, is that a parameter query lets the person running the query specify the criterion Access uses to decide whether or not to return a specific record. You can add a message to the criteria entry dialog box that lets the searcher know what kind of value to enter.

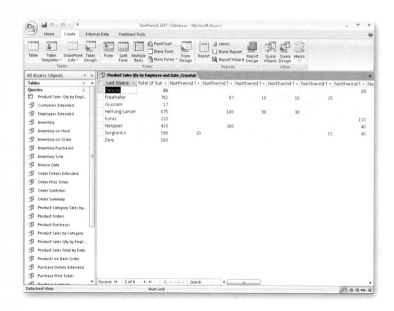

A separate type of query is the *action query*, which makes changes to the physical makeup of your database. You see two types of action queries in this chapter: the *update query*, which lets you change values in a table; and the *make-table query*, which writes query results to a new table in the current database (or another database entirely).

The final query type discussed in this section is the *crosstab query*. Unlike a select query, which presents its results in a datasheet, a crosstab query presents its results in a layout like that of a spreadsheet. Every value in the body of the query's results is related to two other values. In this case, your suppliers and your product categories.

As in a spreadsheet, you can choose the mathematical operation Access uses to summarize the data in the body of the crosstab query's results. Available operations include finding a sum, average, the number of occurrences (as in the crosstab query results shown previously), or even the minimum or maximum value.

Once you create a query (as shown below), you can run it by double-clicking the query's icon in the Database window. If the query is open in Design view, you can run it by clicking the Run button on the Design tab.

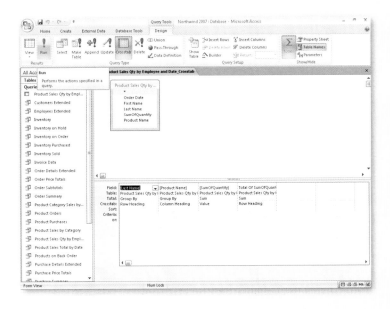

Creating a Query Using the Query Wizard

When you create a basic select query, you identify the table (or tables) with the data you want to find, name the fields to appear in the query results, and then save the query. The Query Wizard walks you through the process, making it easy to identify the tables and fields to appear in your query. What's more, you can choose whether to have Access display detailed results (that is, the individual query rows) or summarize the query's contents.

Create a Detail Query

1. Click the Create tab.
2. Click Query Wizard.
3. Click Simple Query Wizard.
4. Click OK.
5. Click the Tables/Queries down arrow, and then click the table or query with the fields you want to use in your query.

(continued on the next page)

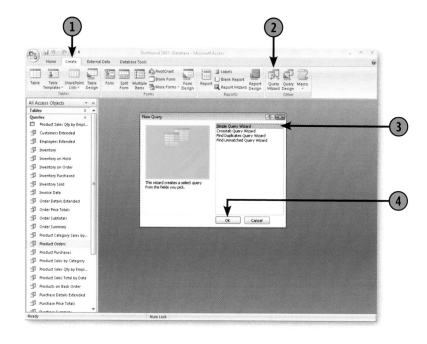

To add all of a table's fields to your query, click the Add All (>>) button. You can also remove a field by clicking the Remove (<) button, or remove all fields by clicking the Remove All (<<) button.

This step of the wizard only appears for some types of queries; don't panic if you don't see it.

Create a Detail Query *(continued)*

6 Click the first field to include in the query's results.

7 Click Add.

8 Repeat steps 6 and 7 to add more fields (and step 5 to change the table or query from which you draw fields).

9 Click Next.

10 Click the Detail option button.

11 Click Next.

12 Type a name for your query.

13 Click Finish.

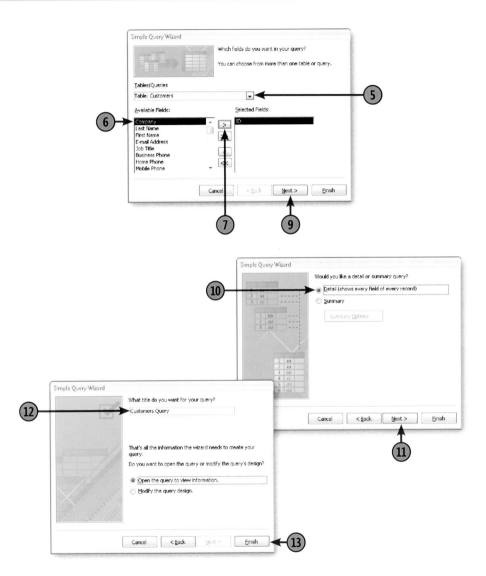

Create a Summary Query

① Click the Create tab.

② Click Query Wizard.

③ Click Simple Query Wizard.

④ Click OK.

⑤ Click the Tables/Queries down arrow, and then click the table or query with the fields you want to use in your query.

⑥ Click the first field to include in the query's results.

⑦ Click Add.

⑧ Repeat steps 6 and 7 to add more fields (and step 5 to change the table or query from which you draw fields).

⑨ Click Next.

(continued on the next page)

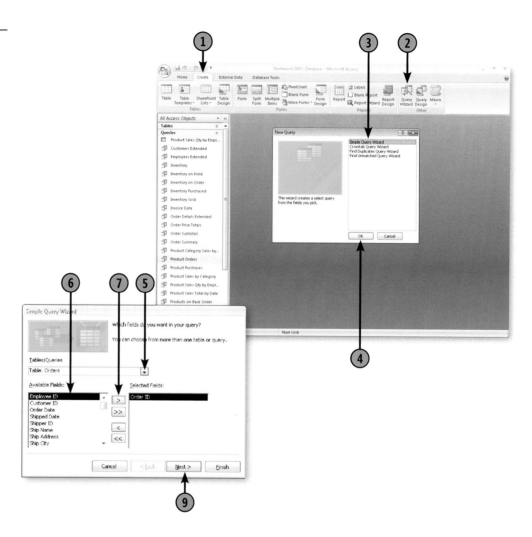

Create a Summary Query *(continued)*

⑩ Click the Summary option button.

⑪ Click Summary Options.

⑫ Select the check boxes representing the summary values you want calculated.

⑬ Click OK.

⑭ Click Next.

⑮ Select the option button representing how you want the query to group rows in the query's source table.

⑯ Click Next.

⑰ Type a name for your query.

⑱ Click Finish.

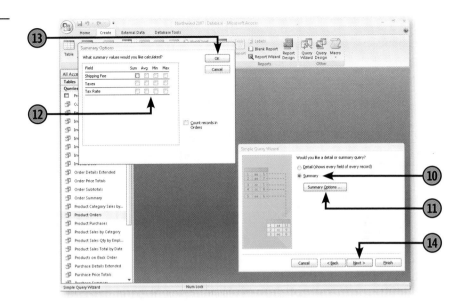

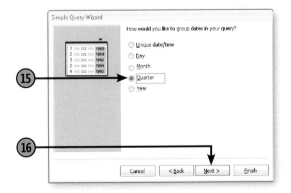

Editing a Query in Design View

After you create a query, you can modify it by opening it in Design view. In Design view, you can add a table to the Query design area, add or remove query fields, or even add every field from a table in one fell swoop.

Open a Query for Editing

① Display the queries in your workbook.

② Right-click a query.

③ Click Design View.

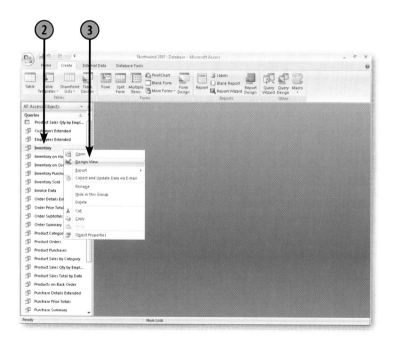

Add a Table to a Query

① Open the query in Design view.

② Click the Show Table button.

③ Click the table to add.

④ Click Add.

⑤ Click Close.

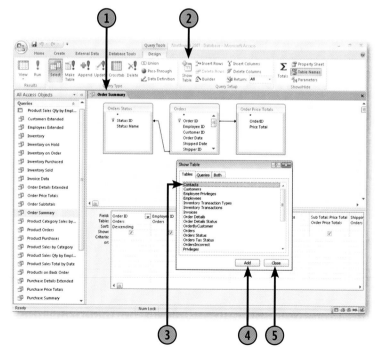

Add a Field to a Query

① Open the query in Design view.

② Drag a field to a Field cell.

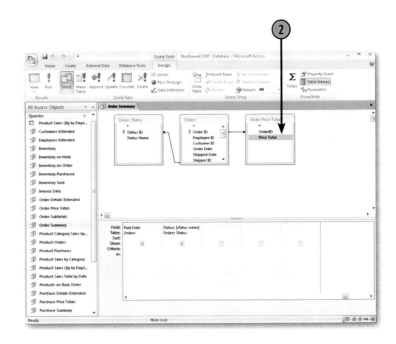

Tip

To add every field from a table to a query's results, drag the asterisk from the table's box in the table area to a Field cell in the query design grid.

Tip

For a query with more than one table to return meaningful results, the two tables must be linked by a relationship.

Create a Query in Design View

1. Click the Create tab.

2. Click Query Design.

3. Click the first table or query you want to add.

4. Click Add.

5. Repeat steps 3 and 4 to add all of the desired tables.

6. Click Close.

7. Drag fields to the design grid.

8. Click the Save button.

9. Type a name for the query.

10. Click OK.

Tip

To remove a table from the design grid, right-click the table's title bar and then click Remove Table.

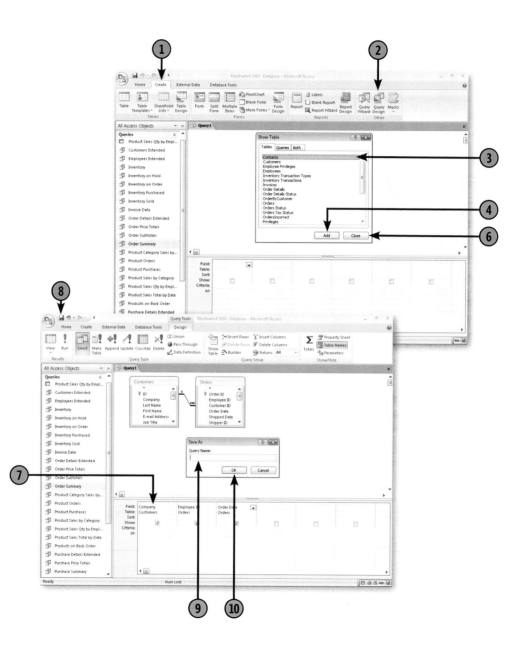

Using Criteria to Focus Query Results

It's likely you won't want your query to find every record in a table—if you did, you could just open the table and not bother with the query! To limit the records a query locates, such as only finding customers in Germany, you can add criteria to the fields in the Query design grid.

Set Query Criteria

1 Open a query in Design view.

2 Click the Criteria cell for the field to which the criterion will be applied.

3 Click Builder.

4 Create the criterion in the Expression Builder.

5 Click OK.

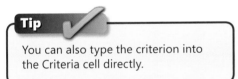

Tip

You can also type the criterion into the Criteria cell directly.

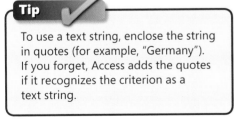

Tip

To use a text string, enclose the string in quotes (for example, "Germany"). If you forget, Access adds the quotes if it recognizes the criterion as a text string.

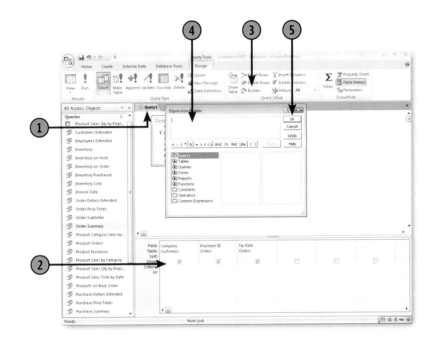

Introducing Operators

There are several types of database objects and tools you need to use when you create a criterion to narrow the records returned by a query or to calculate a value. The first set of objects to which you need to refer includes database tables and their fields. For example, to calculate the subtotal of a line in the Northwind sample database's Order Details table, multiply the Unit Price by the Quantity ordered, and adjust the total if the customer gets a discount (as noted in the Discount field). The expression to perform the first part of that calculation is [Order Details]![UnitPrice]*[Order Details]![Quantity].

Note that table fields are called out with the name of the table enclosed in square brackets, an exclamation point, and then the name of the field in square brackets.

Comparison Operators

Operator	Description
<	Less than
<=	Less than or equal to
<>	Not equal to
=	Equals
>=	Greater than or equal to
>	Greater than
Between "Value1" And "Value2"	Between two values, inclusive (for example, Between "1" And "3" would return, "1, 2, 3")

Arithmetic Operators

Operator	Description
-	Subtraction (6-4=2)
*	Multiplication (6*4=24)
/	Division (6/4=1.5)
\	Integer division (6\4=1)
+	Addition (6+4=10)
Mod	Modular division (6 Mod 4=2)

Logical Operators

Operator	Description
AND	Both elements of an expression must be true.
NOT	The expression must evaluate as false.
OR	At least one element of an expression must be true.
XOR	Exactly one element of an expression must be true, not both.

Using Queries to Calculate Values

One popular use for database tables is to maintain sales records with fields for the order identifier, the product ordered, and the product's price. What you can't do in a table is perform a calculation—the fields are just designed to hold data. In a query, however, you can find totals, averages, or even the minimum or maximum value in the records found by your query.

Calculate a Value in a Query

(1) Open a query in Design view.

(2) Click Totals to add the Total row to the query design grid.

(3) Click the Field cell in the column where you want to calculate the value.

(4) Click Builder.

(5) Build the calculation in the Expression Builder.

(6) Click OK.

(7) In the Field cell with the calculation, edit the value to the left of the colon to reflect the name you want for the field when the query results are displayed as a datasheet.

(8) Click Run.

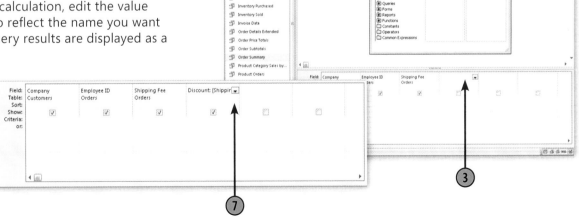

Finding Duplicate Records

The standard select query locates records that meet a criterion, such as orders made by a particular customer during a given month. However, you might also be interested in finding those customers who placed more than one order in a month. If all orders for a month are recorded in the same table, you could create a Find Duplicates query to locate CustomerID values that occur more than once in the table.

Create a Find Duplicates Query

1. Click the Create tab.
2. Click Query Wizard.
3. Click Find Duplicates Query Wizard.
4. Click OK.
5. Click the table in which you want to find duplicate information.
6. Click Next.

(continued on the next page)

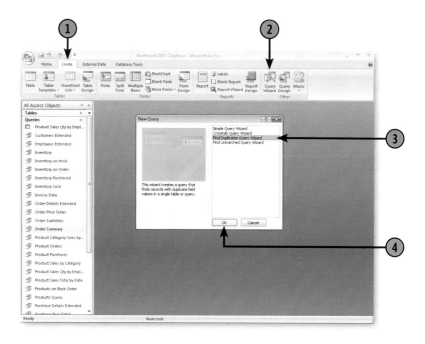

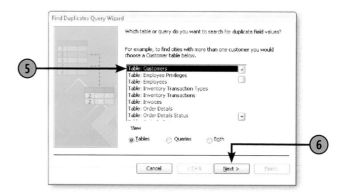

Create a Find Duplicates Query *(continued)*

⑦ Click the field that might contain duplicate information.

⑧ Click Add.

⑨ Repeat steps 7 and 8 to add any other fields to the query.

⑩ Click Next.

⑪ Click any other field to display in the query results.

⑫ Click Add.

⑬ Repeat steps 11 and 12 as necessary.

⑭ Click Next.

⑮ Type a name for the query.

⑯ Click Finish.

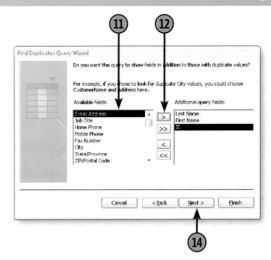

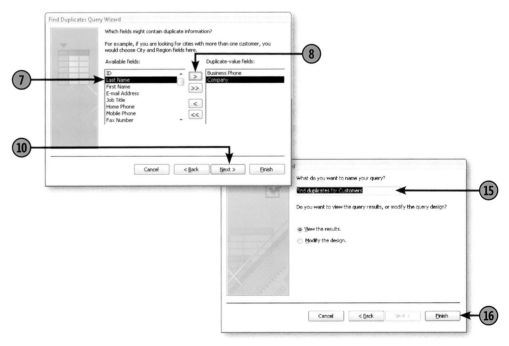

Finding Unmatched Records

When two tables are in a one-to-many relationship, you can create a Find Unmatched Records query to identify any records in the table on the "one" side that have no corresponding records in the table on the "many" side. For example, in the Northwind sample database, because the Customers and Orders tables are in a one-to-many relationship, you could identify customers that have never placed an order.

Create a Find Unmatched Records Query

(1) Click the Create tab.

(2) Click Query Wizard.

(3) Click Find Unmatched Query Wizard.

(4) Click OK.

(5) Click the table in which you want to find unmatched records.

(6) Click Next.

(7) Click the table or query with related records.

(8) Click Next.

(continued on the next page)

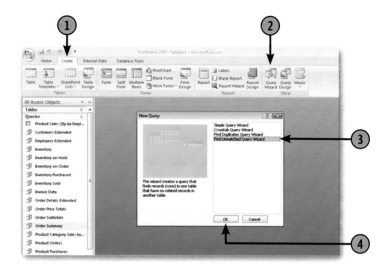

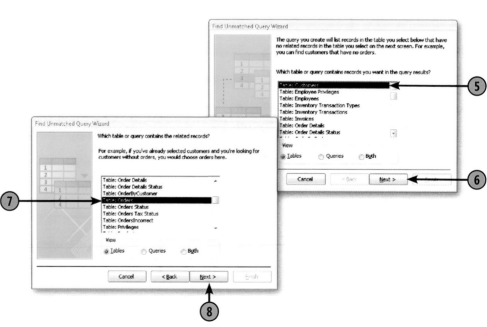

Create a Find Unmatched Records Query (continued)

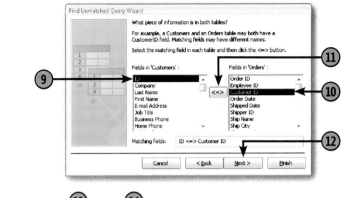

⑨ If necessary, click the field in the left pane that is in the table on the "one" side of the relationship.

⑩ If necessary, click the field in the right pane that is in the table on the "many" side of the relationship.

⑪ Click the Match button to identify the equivalent fields.

⑫ Click Next.

⑬ Click the name of a field to display in the query results.

⑭ Click Add.

⑮ Repeat steps 13 and 14 as needed to add fields to the display.

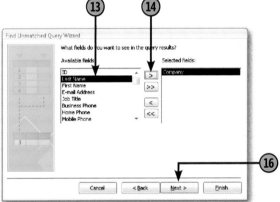

⑯ Click Next.

⑰ Type a name for the query.

⑱ Click Finish.

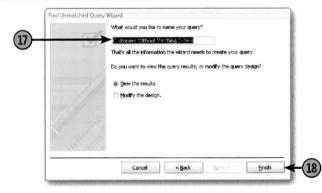

Try This!

Open the Northwind sample database, click the Create tab, click the Query Wizard button, and then double-click Find Unmatched Query Wizard. Click Table: Customers and then click Next. In the next screen, click Table: Orders and then click Next. Verify that ID is highlighted in the Customers table and that CustomerID is highlighted in the Orders table and click Next. Click Company, click the Add button, and then click Next. In the final screen, click Finish to accept the query name Access suggests. The query you create displays customers that have not placed an order.

Writing Query Results to a New Table

When you run a query, Access writes the records the query finds into a dynaset, or dynamic record set. While Access remembers the results of queries you run, the results aren't actually writ-ten to a table, limiting what you can do with the data. You can, however, modify a select query so the results are written to a new table.

Create a Make-Table Query

1. Open a query in Design view.

2. Click Make Table.

3. Type a name for the new table.

4. Click OK.

5. Click Run.

6. Click Yes to create a new table that contains the selected records.

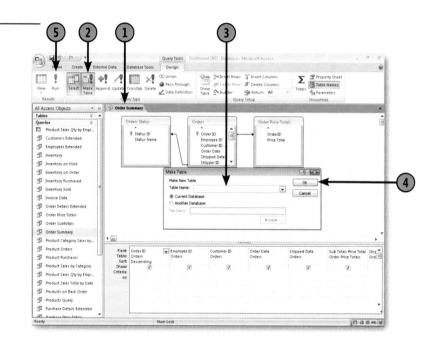

Creating an Update Query

One exciting aspect of business is how quickly things change—of course, it can be difficult to keep track of all those changes! One useful task you can perform with an Update query is to modify values in a table to reflect changes in your business environment. For example, if a supplier increases prices by 5 percent, you can create an Update query that moves through your Products table and updates the records for that supplier's products.

Update Table Values with a Query

1. Open a query in Design view.

2. Click Update.

3. In the Criteria cell of the column you'll use to select the records to update, type the expression used to select which values should be updated.

4. In the Update To cell of the column that contains the value to be updated, type the expression used to update the values.

5. Click Run.

See Also

For more information about ensuring table data is updated to reflect changes in a related table, see "Enforcing Referential Integrity" on page 48.

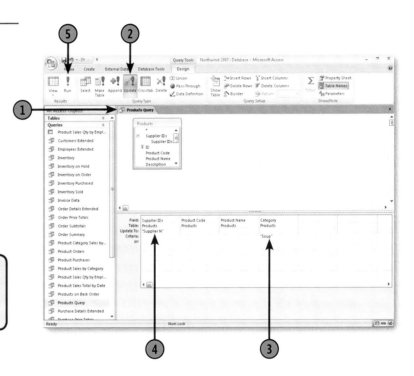

Creating a Crosstab Query

The basic means of storing and presenting data in Access is the table, which is essentially a list of information about a group of "things" (such as customer orders) related to a single primary key value. Another way to present data is in a Crosstab query, which relates one value (such as a total or average) with two other values (such as a customer and a month).

Build a Crosstab Query

1 Click the Create tab.

2 Click Query Wizard.

3 Click Crosstab Query Wizard.

4 Click OK.

5 Click the table or query to provide the values for your crosstab query.

6 Click Next.

7 Click the field to provide values for the row headings.

8 Click Add.

9 Click Next.

(continued on the next page)

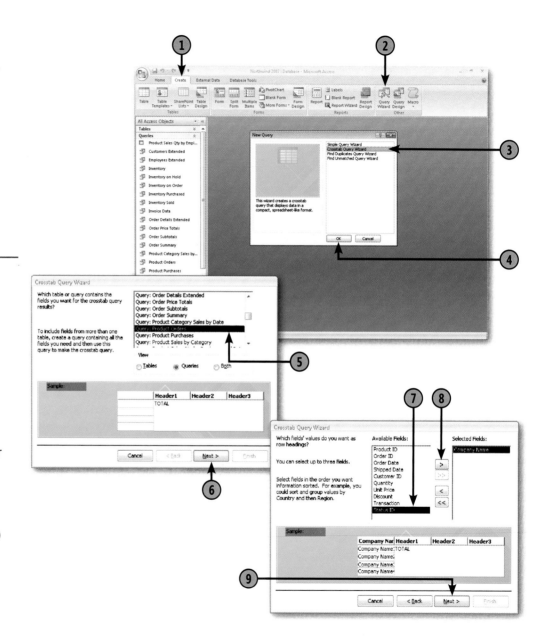

Build a Crosstab Query *(continued)*

10 Click the field to provide values for the column headings.

11 Click Next.

12 Click the field to provide values for the data area (body) of the crosstab query.

13 Click the summary calculation to be performed on the values in the data area.

14 Click Next.

15 Type a name for the query.

16 Click Finish.

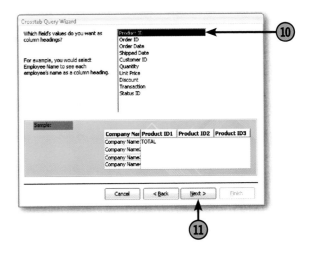

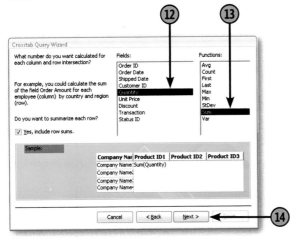

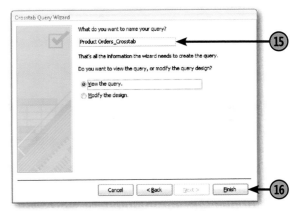

Finding the Largest and Smallest Values in a Field by Using a Query

When you create a query, you can have Access display a set number of the highest and lowest values in the query's results. You can also have Access display rows that contain the top or bottom values by asking Access to display a certain percentage of rows in the query's results. For example, if you reward the top 10 percent of your sales staff, you can create a query that sorts the query results according to the values in the

Total Sales field and display the best values. When you filter a query's results by a percentage, you don't need to know the exact number of records in your table. In other words, if your sales staff expands from 30 to 40 employees, creating a query that displays the top 10 percent displays the top four sales representatives, rather than the top three, without you having to edit the query.

Find the Largest Values in a Field

1. Open a query in Design view.

2. Click the Sort cell of the field in which you want to find the top values.

3. Click the down arrow that appears.

4. Click Descending.

5. If necessary, click the Design tab.

6. In the Top Values field, type one of these two types of values:

   ■ Type a number indicating the number of values you want displayed in the query results.

   ■ Type a percentage indicating the portion of the table's rows you want displayed in the query results.

7. Click Run.

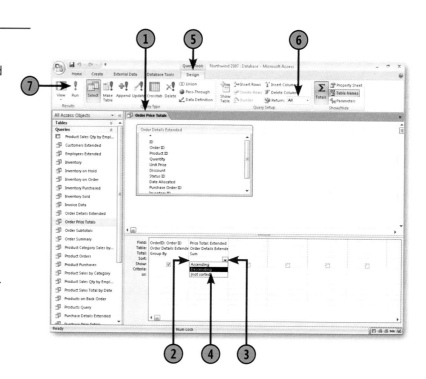

Find the Smallest Values in a Field

① Open a query in Design view.

② Click the Sort cell of the field in which you want to find the top values.

③ Click the down arrow that appears.

④ Click Ascending.

⑤ If necessary, click the Design tab.

⑥ In the Top Values field, type one of these two types of values:

   ■ Type a number indicating the number of values you want displayed in the query results.

   ■ Type a percentage indicating the portion of the table's rows you want displayed in the query results.

⑦ Click Run.

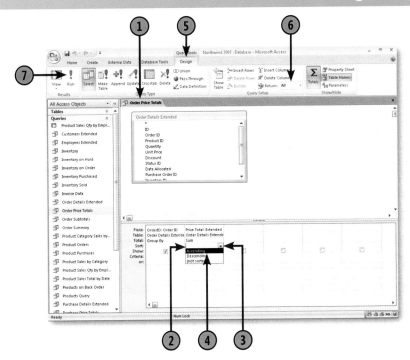

Tip

To have your query display all of its results, return to Design view, click the Design tab, click the Top Values field's down arrow, and then click All.

10

Creating Reports

Reports give you the ability to present your table and query data in an accessible format. In some ways, reports and forms are very similar—both types of database objects let you display your table records and query results at one record per page, in a series of columns or rows, or in a custom layout you create in Design view. The difference between forms and reports is that in addition to presenting your table and query data, reports let you summarize your data. For example, you can create a report that not only lists every order made by every customer, but also finds the total amount of all orders for a particular customer. It's possible to do the same thing with queries, but the Report Wizard streamlines the process greatly, saving you time and effort while producing valuable information.

Creating a Report Using the Report Wizard

Although it might be possible to generate useful reports from the data in a single table or query, it's very likely that you'll want to combine data from more than one table or query into a single report. For example, you might have product data in a single report. For example, you might have product data in one table and supplier data in another table, and then want to create a report where full supplier contact information accompanies the product information. You can do that by creating a report using the Report Wizard.

Step through the Report Wizard

1. Click the Create tab.

2. Click Report Wizard.

3. Click the down arrow and then choose the first table or query from which you want to draw values for the report.

4. Click a field in the Available Fields box and then click either of the following buttons:

   - Add to add the selected field.

   - Add All to add all fields to the report.

5. Click Next.

   - If you created a report based on a query that reads in primary key values from more than one table, a wizard page appears asking you to select a preliminary grouping criteria for the report's records. Click the name of the field by which you want to group and then click Next.

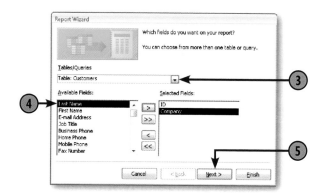

(continued on the next page)

Step through the Report Wizard *(continued)*

6 If necessary, click the first field by which you want to group the report's contents and then click Add. Repeat to add grouping levels.

7 Click Next.

8 Click the first field's down arrow, and click the first field by which you want to sort the report's contents.

9 If necessary, click the sort options to toggle between Ascending or Descending.

10 Click Next.

11 Use the controls on the remaining wizard pages to select a layout, page orientation, style, and name for the report. When you're done, click Finish.

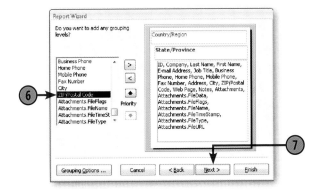

Tip

You can remove fields from the Selected Fields pane of the Report Wizard by clicking the field name and then clicking either Remove, to remove the selected field, or clicking Remove All, to remove all fields.

See Also

For information about changing report grouping levels, see "Grouping Report Records" on page 135.

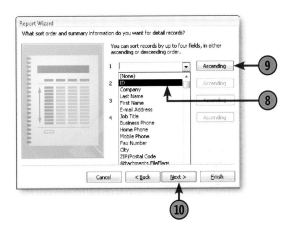

Creating a Summary Report

Although both database object types let you display your table and query records, one thing you can do in a report that you can't with a form is to summarize your data within a report. For example, if you created a summary report of all orders and grouped the report's contents by product, you could add a summary function to find the total sales for each product. You could also find the minimum, maximum, or average value of orders for each listed product.

Build a Summary Report

① Click the Create tab.

② Click Report Wizard.

③ Click the down arrow, and then choose the first table or query from which you want to draw values for the report.

④ Click a field in the Available Fields box, and then click either of the following buttons:

- Add to add the selected field.

- Add All to add all fields to the report.

⑤ Click Next.

- If you created a report based on a query that reads in primary key values from more than one table, a wizard page appears asking you to select a preliminary grouping criteria for the report's records. Click the name of the field by which you want to group and then click Next.

⑥ Click the first field by which you want to group the report's contents and then click Add. Repeat to add grouping levels.

⑦ Click Next.

(continued on the next page)

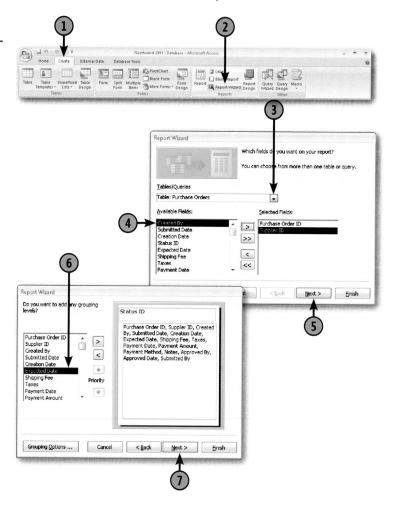

Build a Summary Report *(continued)*

8 Click the first field's down arrow and click the first field by which you want to sort the report's contents.

9 Click the sort options button to toggle between Ascending or Descending.

10 Click Summary Options.

11 Select the check box representing the target field and summary operation.

12 Select the option indicating whether to display the summary alone or details (report rows) and the summary.

13 Click OK.

14 Click Next.

15 Use the controls on the remaining wizard pages to select a layout, page orientation, style, and name for the report. Click Finish when you're done.

Tip

You can select more than one field and summary function—every summary you choose will appear in your finished report.

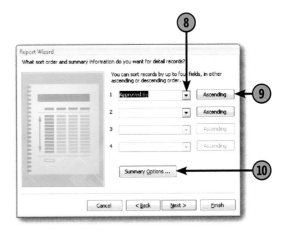

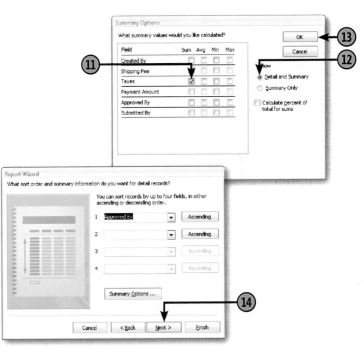

Creating a Report in Design View

The Report Wizard makes it easy to create reports, but you can also create a blank form in Design view and start adding controls on your own. If the report will consist only of a few fields and you want to place the fields in particular locations, you might want to create the report in Design view, rather than creating it using a wizard and then editing the result in Design view. Of course, you might just prefer working in Design view!

Build a New Report

① Click the Create tab.

② Click Report Design.

③ In the Field List task pane, click the show detail control next to the table to provide fields or the report.

④ Drag fields from the Field List task pane to the report's Detail section.

⑤ Click Save.

⑥ Type a name for the report.

⑦ Click OK.

Try This!

In the Northwind sample database, click the Create tab and then click Report Design. Click Add Existing Fields, and click the show detail control next to the Products table. Drag the Product Name, Description, and List Price fields to the form's Detail section. Click Save, type a name for the report, and then click OK.

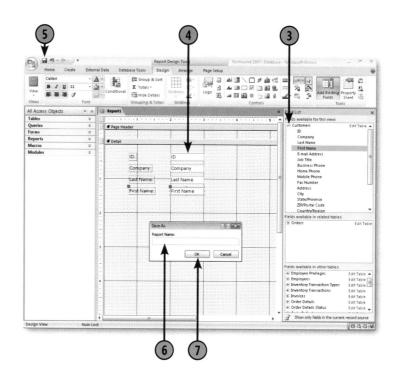

Modifying an Existing Report

Once you create a report, you can open it in Design view and add or remove fields. The available fields appear in the Field List task pane; to add a field, just drag its name from the Field List task pane to the body of the report.

Open a Report for Editing

① Display the database's reports in the Navigation Pane.

② Right-click a report.

③ Click Design View.

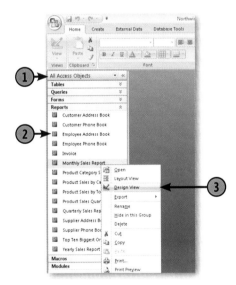

Tip

When you have a report open in Design view, you can also display the Field List task pane by pressing Alt+F8.

See Also

For more information about modifying reports, see "Beautifying Forms and Reports" on page 143.

Display or Hide the Field List Task Pane

■ Click Add Existing Fields to display or hide the Field List task pane.

Add a Field to a Report

① Drag the field from the Field List task pane to the desired spot on the form.

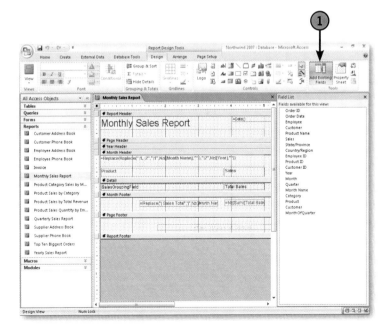

Adding and Deleting Report Controls

After you create a report, you can add controls like labels, text boxes, check boxes, and option buttons to display your table and query data. The specific steps you take to add a control and define its data source depend on the control you want to create, but the Control Wizards are there to help you through the process.

When you create a control, you actually create a control (such as a text box) and a label identifying the control. You can delete, modify, or move the label without affecting its associated control.

Add a Control Using a Wizard

① Open a report in Design view.

② If necessary, click the Design tab.

③ If necessary, click Use Control Wizards.

④ Click the control you want to add.

⑤ Drag the mouse pointer on the report to define the control's area.

⑥ Follow the steps in the wizard to define the contents of the control.

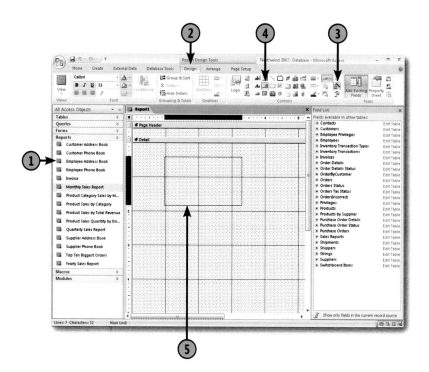

Delete a Control

① Right-click the control you want to delete.

② Click Delete

See Also

For more information about controls and control types, see the table "Available Control Types" on page 96.

Modify Control Properties

① Open the report in Design view.

② Click the control.

③ Click Property Sheet.

④ Click the property to change.

⑤ Follow one of these steps:

■ Type a new value in the text box next to the property name.

■ Click the down arrow, and select a new property from the list that appears.

■ Click the Build button, and use the dialog box that appears to select or construct a new value.

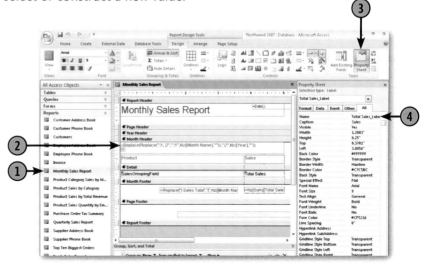

Tip

When you delete a control, be sure to click the control itself—not the label next to the control.

Tip

You can change the value in a control's label by editing the label directly or by setting the control's Caption property.

Calculating Values in a Report

When you create a report, you can create a control (such as a text box) that performs a calculation on the values elsewhere in the report. For example, if a report record had a field for a product's Price and another field noting the Quantity ordered, you can create a control that multiplies the values from those fields and displays the result. Creating calculated fields in a report is handy when you work with a popular query and you don't want Access to recalculate the values every time the query is run.

Create a Calculated Field

1. Open a report in Design view.

2. If necessary, click the Design tab.

3. Click the Text Box control.

4. In the report Detail section, drag to define the area for the text box.

5. Click the Property Sheet button.

6. If necessary, click the Data tab.

7. In the Control Source field, type = followed by the expression used to calculate the field's value and then press Tab.

8. Type a new value for the text box's label.

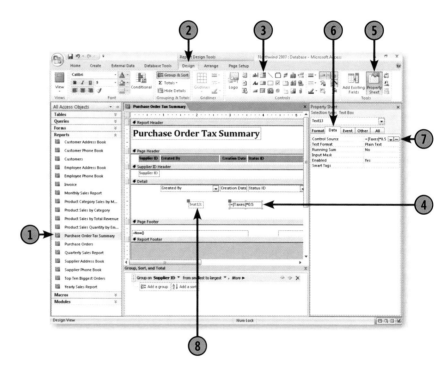

See Also

For information about calculating summary values in a report, as opposed to calculating a value based on the current record, see "Creating a Summary Report" on page 128.

Tip

Clicking the Build button to the right of the Control Source property opens the Expression Builder.

Introducing Report Sections

A basic report has five sections:

- Report Header
- Page Header
- Detail
- Page Footer
- Report Footer

The Report Header section holds information that appears at the top of the first page of the printed report. Typical information you find in the Report Header includes the title of the report, the logo of the company producing the report, and the report's author.

The Page Header, by contrast, contains information that appears at the top of every printed report page. Most frequently, you find the report's column headings, page numbers, and dates in this report area, but you can also put smaller versions of a company logo in this area to identify the report's origins. If the report data is confidential, this area (and the Report Header) is a good place to note that, as the annotation appears on every page.

The Page Footer and Report Footer sections are the complement of the Page Header and Report Header sections. Information in the Page Footer section appears at the bottom of every printed report page, while information in the Report Footer section appears at the bottom of the last printed report page.

The report's Detail section is where the table records or query results appear. Whether the Detail section has one or more than one record depends on how you set up your report. As with any report section, you can add other controls, text, or drawing objects to make your data easier to comprehend.

If you add a grouping level to a report, Access lets you add a header and footer section named after the field used to group the report's contents. For example, if you group the contents of a report based on a query combining data from the Customers, Orders, and Order Details tables, you could group the report's contents by the country of the customer. If you did, two sections named Country Header and Country Footer would appear in the report, flanking the Detail section.

Grouping Report Records

When you create a report using the Report Wizard, you can define how the report's records are grouped. For example, you can create a report based on the Northwind sample database's Orders and Order Details tables and group records by Customer ID. If you want to display each customer's orders by the date they were placed, you can create a second grouping level based on the Order Date field.

When you add a grouping level to a report, Access adds a header corresponding to the grouping field's name. If you group a set of products by their category name, Access creates a CategoryName Header; if you like, you can add a Category-Name Footer as well.

Create a Grouping Level

① Open a report in Layout view.

② Click the Formatting tab.

③ In the Grouping & Totals group, click Group & Sort.

④ Click Add A Group.

⑤ Click the field by which you want to group the report's contents.

⑥ If desired, click the second down arrow in the group description, and change the sort order from With A on Top (ascending order) to With Z on Top (descending order).

⑦ Click More.

⑧ Click the Without a Footer Section down arrow.

⑨ Click With a Footer Section.

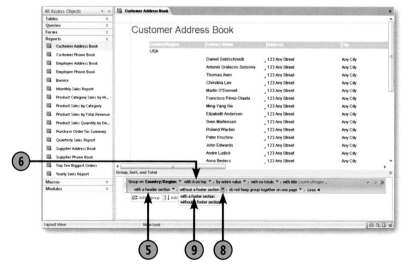

Reorder Grouping Levels

① Open a grouped report in Layout view.

② Click the Formatting tab.

③ If necessary, click Group & Sort.

④ Click the grouping level you want to move.

⑤ Follow either of these steps:

▪ Click the Move Up button to move the grouping level higher in the order.

▪ Click the Move Down button to move the grouping level down in the order.

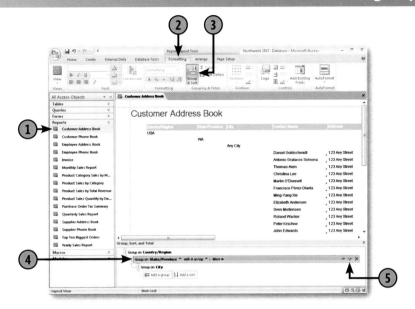

Delete a Grouping Level

① Open a grouped report in Layout view.

② Click the Formatting tab.

③ If necessary, click Group & Sort.

④ Click the grouping level you want to delete.

⑤ Click the Delete button.

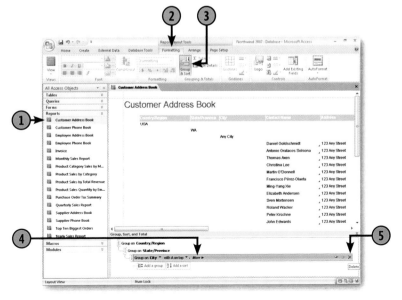

Creating a Subreport

An Access database often has a number of relationships between tables. In the Northwind sample database, for example, Suppliers make Products, which are part of Orders placed by Customers. When two tables are in a one-to-many relationship, you can create a report based on the contents of the table on the "one" side of the relationship and add a subreport displaying related records from the table on the "many" side of the relationship. The Customers and Orders tables are in a one-to-many relationship (they have the Customer ID field in common), so you could create a report listing every customer and add a subreport displaying all orders placed by the current customer.

Add a Subreport

① Open a report in Design view.

② Click the Subform/Subreport control.

③ In the Detail section of the report, drag to define the area where the subreport should appear.

④ Select the Use An Existing Report Or Form option.

⑤ Click the report or form to supply the data for the subreport.

⑥ Click Next.

(continued on the next page)

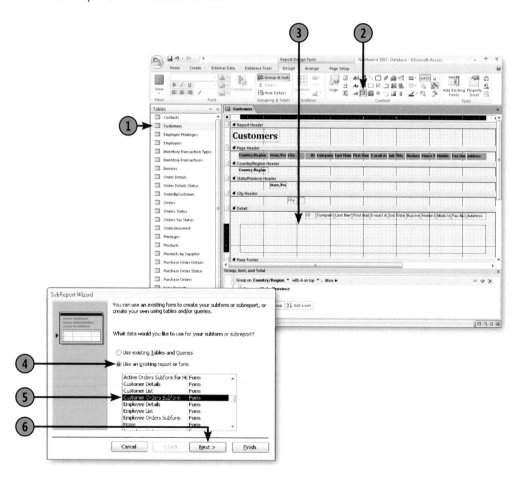

Add a Subreport *(continued)*

⑦ Click the relationship from which Access should create the subreport.

⑧ Click Next.

⑨ Type Subreport after the end of the suggested subreport name.

⑩ Click Finish.

See Also

For more information about relationships, see "Creating Relationships between Tables" on page 46.

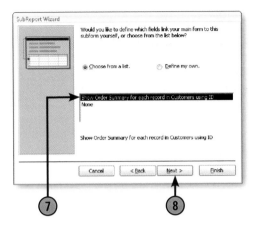

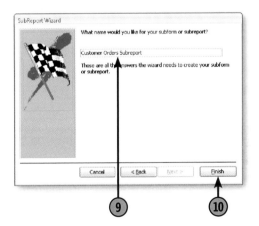

Creating Mailing Labels

One frequent use for contact information in a database is to create a set of mailing labels so you can send special offers or notes of appreciation to all or a subset of your customers or suppliers. The Label Wizard walks you through the process, letting you choose the type of label on which you print, pick the table and query fields you want printed on the labels, and add any punctuation or other text to each label.

Generate Mailing Labels

(1) Click the database object from which you want to create your mailing labels.

(2) Click the Create tab.

(3) Click Labels.

(4) Click the label size you want to print onto.

(5) Click Next to accept the default font settings.

(continued on the next page)

See Also

For more information about how grouping and sorting affects the order of records on a report, see "Grouping Report Records" on page 135.

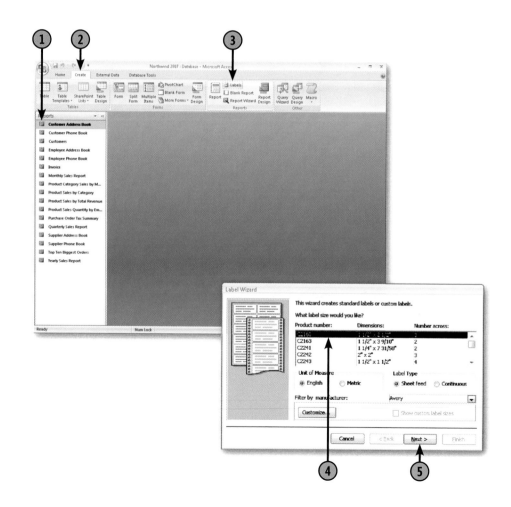

Generate Mailing Labels *(continued)*

⑥ Click the first field to appear on the label.

⑦ Click Add.

⑧ Click the position on the label for the next field.

■ Repeat steps 6 to 8 to add all desired fields to the label.

⑨ If desired, type any text (such as punctuation) you want to appear on the label.

⑩ Click Next.

⑪ Click the first field to use as the sort criteria for the labels.

⑫ Click Add.

■ Repeat steps 11 and 12 to add additional sort criteria.

⑬ Click Next.

⑭ Type a name for the report and click Finish.

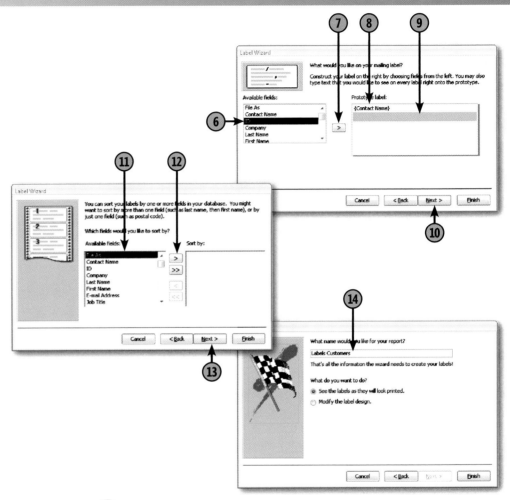

Tip

You should always print one test page of mailing labels on regular paper to be sure everything lines up correctly and looks the way you want it to.

Tip

Line breaks aren't accepted in the Label Wizard. To position text on the label's next line, click the line.

Beautifying Forms and Reports

After you create forms and reports to display your table and query data, you can change the appearance of any control on the form or report. You can change the appearance of individual elements in your Microsoft Office Access objects, but an easier way to change the format of an entire document at once is to use an AutoFormat that is included with Access. You can use an AutoFormat as it is out of the box, or you can choose to apply certain parts of the AutoFormat. If you want, you can even create and modify your own AutoFormats so you can make the appearance of your forms and reports consistent.

Another useful Access capability is to create a conditional format, which changes the appearance of the data in a text box based on the data's value. If a customer hasn't placed an order in the last year, a product has been discontinued, or a shipment took more than a week to arrive, you can use conditional formats to highlight that data and bring it to your attention quickly.

Formatting Text

Access is a great program for storing your data efficiently, but it also gives you a lot of flexibility in choosing how to display data in forms and reports. One important part of designing a form or report is choosing formats for each element of the design: labels, headings, and data. Corporate logos, color schemes, and documents can help guide initial development, but you should always listen to your colleagues to discover ways to make the text on your forms and reports easier to understand. Opening a form or report in Design view lets you make your changes, but feel free to switch between Design view and either Form view or Print Preview (for reports) to see how your changes will look in the finished document.

Change Text Formatting

① Select the text to be formatted.

② Click the Home tab.

③ Use the ribbon buttons in the Font group to format your text.

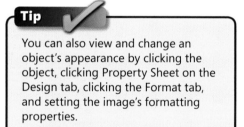

Tip

You can also view and change an object's appearance by clicking the object, clicking Property Sheet on the Design tab, clicking the Format tab, and setting the image's formatting properties.

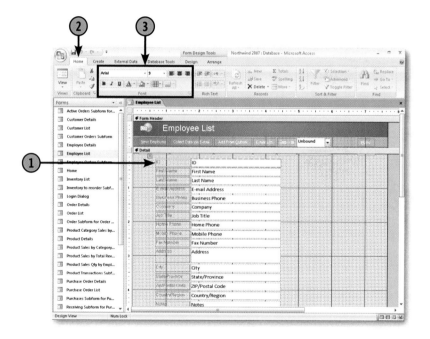

Applying AutoFormats

Rather than define the format of every object in your forms and reports, you can apply one of the AutoFormats installed with Access. AutoFormats let you do more than just apply an existing format, however; you can choose which elements of an AutoFormat to apply, create new AutoFormats to match the formatting of an existing form or report, or modify an existing AutoFormat.

Select an AutoFormat

① Open the form or report you want to format in Design view.

② Click the Arrange tab.

③ Click AutoFormat.

④ Click the AutoFormat you want to apply.

Caution

You can't change a built-in AutoFormat; you can only change an AutoFormat you created.

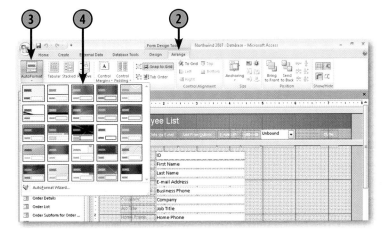

Apply AutoFormat Elements

1 Open the form or report you want to format in Design view.

2 Click the Arrange tab.

3 Click AutoFormat.

4 Click AutoFormat Wizard.

5 Click the AutoFormat you want to apply.

6 Click Options.

7 Select or clear the Font, Color, and Border check boxes to select the AutoFormat attributes you want to apply.

8 Click OK.

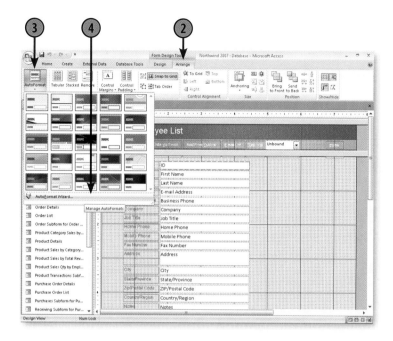

Customize an AutoFormat

1 Open the form or report you want to format in Design view.

2 Click the Arrange tab.

3 Click AutoFormat.

4 Click AutoFormat Wizard.

5 Click the AutoFormat you want to customize. You can only customize an AutoFormat you created.

6 Click Customize.

7 Select the Update option to modify the selected AutoFormat to match the formatting of the active form or report.

8 Click OK to close the Customize AutoFormat dialog box.

9 Click OK to close the AutoFormat dialog box.

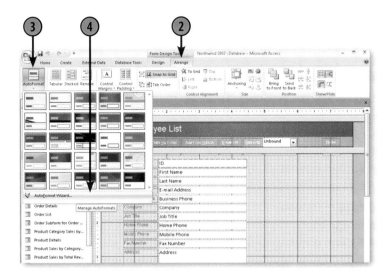

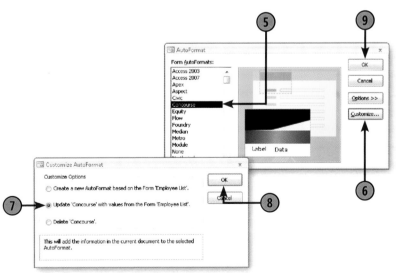

Create an AutoFormat

① Open the form or report you want to format in Design view.

② Click the Arrange tab.

③ Click AutoFormat.

④ Click AutoFormat Wizard.

⑤ Click the AutoFormat you want to customize.

⑥ Click Customize.

⑦ Select the Create A New AutoFormat option and click OK.

⑧ Type the name of the new AutoFormat in the New Style Name dialog box.

⑨ Click OK to close the New Style Name dialog box.

⑩ Click OK to close both the Customize AutoFormat and AutoFormat dialog boxes.

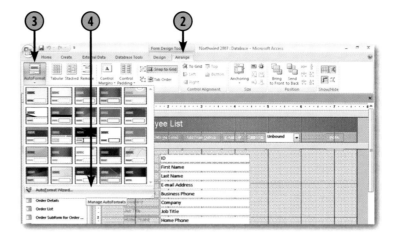

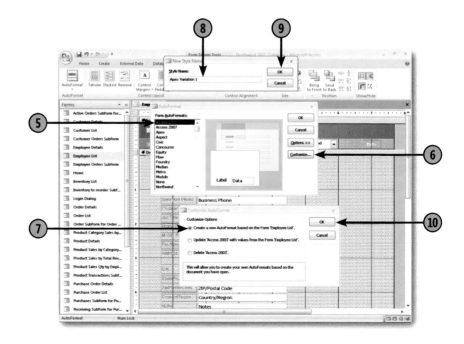

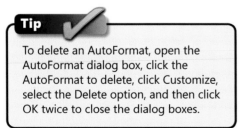

Tip

To delete an AutoFormat, open the AutoFormat dialog box, click the AutoFormat to delete, click Customize, select the Delete option, and then click OK twice to close the dialog boxes.

Setting Control Appearance

Once you add controls to a form or report, you can change the appearance of those controls by displaying the Design tab and using the buttons in the Font group. You can change the color of any control element as well as being able to

apply special effects to the controls, changing how they're drawn on the form or report. You can also use the commands on the ribbon's Arrange tab to arrange and distribute your controls attractively.

Change Control Colors

① Right-click the control you want to format.

② Follow either of these steps:

■ Click the Fill/Back Color menu item, and choose a color for the control's background elements.

■ Click the Font/Fore Color menu item, and choose a color for the control's foreground and text elements.

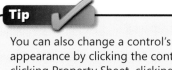

Tip

You can also change a control's appearance by clicking the control, clicking Property Sheet, clicking the Format tab, and changing the control's formatting properties.

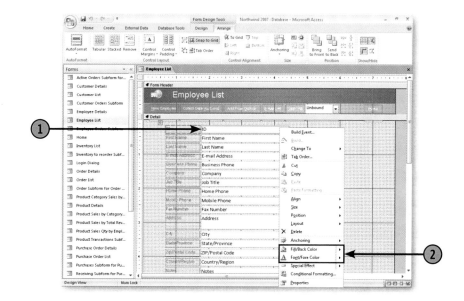

Format Controls with Special Effects

(1) Right-click the control you want to format.

(2) Point to the Special Effect menu item.

(3) Click the effect you want to apply to the control.

Caution

Applying the Etched and Chiseled special effects removes an object's fill and line/border color settings.

Tip

You can change the color of a shadow by changing the object's line color.

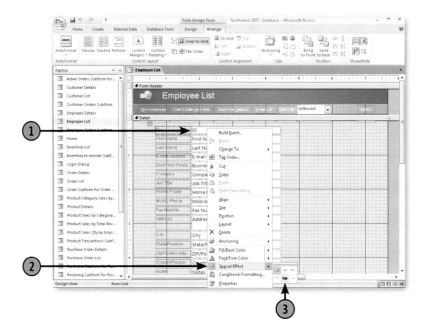

Distribute Controls Horizontally

1. Display the form or report in Design view.

2. Select the controls you want to distribute on the form or report.

3. If necessary, click the Arrange tab.

4. Using the controls in the Position group on the ribbon, follow any of these steps:

   - Click the Make Horizontal Spacing Equal button to space the selected controls evenly.

   - Click the Increase Horizontal Spacing button to push the selected controls farther apart.

   - Click the Decrease Horizontal Spacing button to pull the selected controls closer together.

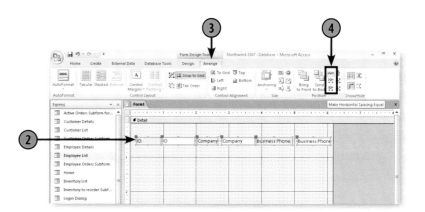

Tip

It's usually a good idea to click the Equal Horizontal button first so your controls will be a uniform distance apart before you use the Increase Horizontal or Decrease Horizontal buttons to change the layout of your controls

Distribute Controls Vertically

① Display the form or report in Design view.

② Select the controls you want to distribute on the form or report.

③ If necessary, click the Arrange tab.

④ Using the controls in the Position group on the ribbon, follow any of these steps:

■ Click the Make Vertical Spacing Equal button to space the selected controls evenly.

■ Click the Increase Vertical Spacing button to push the selected controls farther apart.

■ Click the Decrease Vertical Spacing button to pull the selected controls closer together.

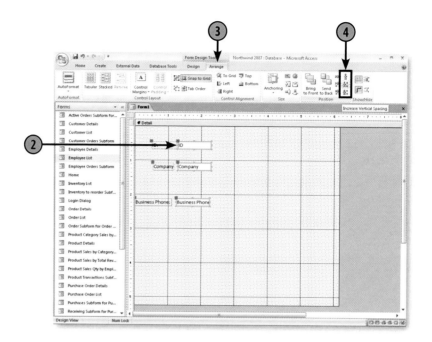

Try This!

Open the Northwind sample database, click Forms on the Shutter Bar, right-click Product Details, and then click Design View. Select the Product Code, Product Name, Description, and Category labels. On the ribbon, click the Arrange tab, and then, in the Position group, click the Decrease Vertical button. The labels move closer together. To return the labels to their previous spacing, click the Increase Vertical button. Click the Close box to close the form.

Align Controls

(1) Select the controls you want to align.

(2) Click the Arrange tab.

(3) Click the control in the Control Alignment group on the ribbon that reflects the alignment you want to apply:

- Click Left to align the selected objects by their left edges.

- Click Right to align the selected objects by their right edges.

- Click Top to align the selected objects by their top edges.

- Click Bottom to align the selected objects by their bottom edges.

- Click To Grid to move each object to the nearest point on the design grid.

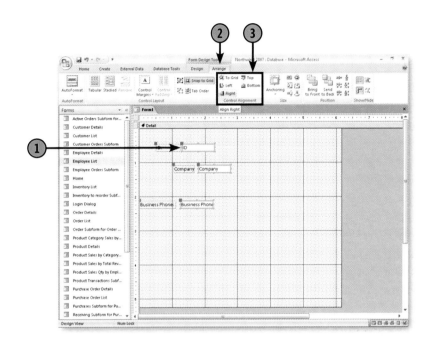

Tip ✔

If you want to help ensure that your objects are aligned, click the Arrange tab on the ribbon and then, in the Control Layout group, click the Snap to Grid button. Turning on the grid limits where you can place your objects; if you want to place an object so it isn't aligned with the design grid, hold down the Ctrl key while you move the object.

Tip ✔

For even more control over your form and report controls' appearance, click the control you want to modify, click the Design tab on the ribbon, click Property Sheet, click the Format tab, and set the properties using the tools in the Property Sheet task pane.

Adding Lines, Shapes, and Borders

When you create a control to display form and report data, you also create a label that you can modify to identify the data presented in the control. Although labels are a great help in identifying the source of your form and report data, they only go so far in identifying groups of controls. For example, if you were to create a report from the contents of a Products table, you could separate general information about a product (such as its category and supplier) from the more specific information by drawing a line between the two groups of controls.

Draw a Line

① Open a form or report in Design view.

② If necessary, click the Design tab.

③ Click the Line control.

④ In the body of the form or report, drag the mouse pointer to create the line.

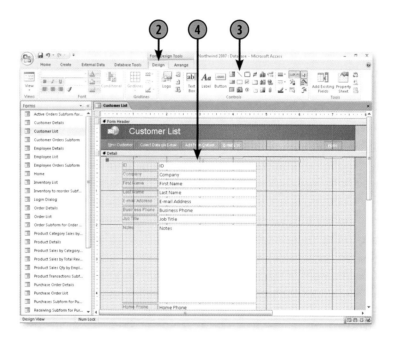

Add a Border

① Open a form or report in Design view.

② Click the control to which you want to add a border.

③ If necessary, click the Design tab.

④ Click the Line Color button's down arrow.

⑤ Click the color you want to apply to the border.

Change an Object's Fill Color

① Open a form or report in Design view.

② Right-click the object.

③ Point to Fill/Back Color.

④ Click the color you want to fill the object.

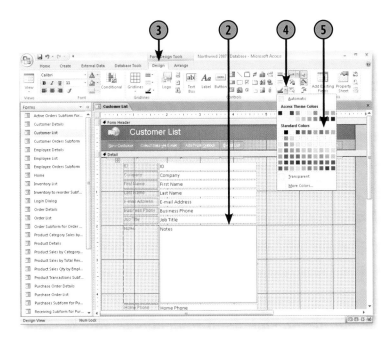

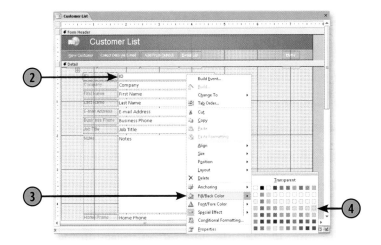

Editing Lines and Borders

After you add a line to a form or report or display a border around a control, you can change the properties of the line or border. You can move, resize, or change the color of a line and change the color of a border.

Resize a Line

① Click either end of the line you want to resize.

② Drag any of the handles surrounding the line to resize the line.

Change Line and Border Color

① Click the line or object you want to change.

② If necessary, click the Design tab.

③ Click the Line Color button down arrow.

④ Click the color you want to apply to the line or border.

Tip

You can repeat your last color selection by clicking the Line Color button—the most recently used color appears on the button's face.

Tip

Dragging the handle at either end of the line lets you move that end of the line freely.

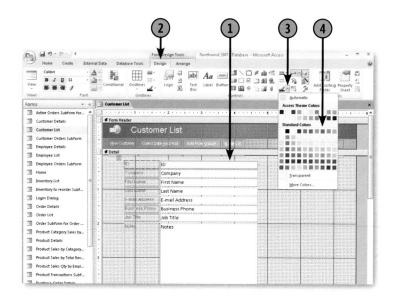

Showing Gridlines in a Report

Access facilitates form and report design by enabling you to "snap" your form and report controls to a grid. When the grid is turned on, Access limits where you can move your controls. Drawing lines through the allowable spots forms a grid of horizontal and vertical lines on your form or report's body. If you'd like to make those gridlines visible on your form or report, you can turn them on quickly. The gridlines are black by default, but you can change their color, line style, and thickness by using the controls in the Gridlines group on the Design tab. Feel free to play around with different gridline appearances until you find the setting combination that looks the best on your form or report.

Turn Gridlines On or Off

① Open a form or report in Design view.

② If necessary, click the Design tab.

③ Click Gridlines.

④ Click the gridline option you want to apply.

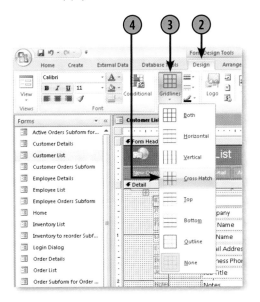

Change Gridline Appearance

① Open a form or report in Design view.

② If necessary, click the Design tab.

③ Follow any of these steps:

▪ Click the Width button and then click the desired gridline width option.

▪ Click the Style button and then click the desired gridline style option.

▪ Click the Color button and then click the desired gridline color.

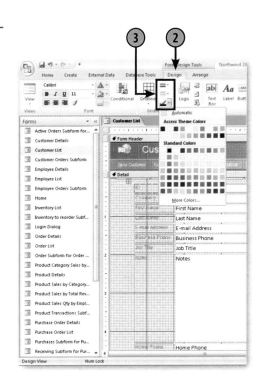

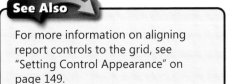

See Also

For more information on aligning report controls to the grid, see "Setting Control Appearance" on page 149.

Coloring Alternate Rows in a Form or Report

You can create forms and reports that display one table or query record per page, but viewing data one record at a time can take away your ability to relate one record to the next. Viewing multiple records on a form or report helps you spot patterns in your data, but distinguishing one row from another can be difficult unless you change the formatting to make the rows stand out from their neighbors. In Access 2007, you can

format your form or report so that alternating data rows have a different background color. You can choose whichever color combinations you'd like, but bear in mind that a combination that works well onscreen might not work well on the printed page. Test your choices to figure out which combinations best meet your needs.

Color Alternate Data Rows

1. Display a form in Datasheet view.
2. Click the Home tab.
3. In the Font group, click the Alternate Fill/Back Color button's down arrow.
4. Click the color you want to apply to alternate datasheet form rows.

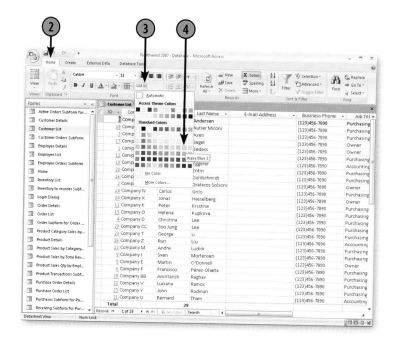

Adding a Totals Row to a Datasheet

Previous versions of Access enabled you to add summary calculations to your reports, but if you viewed your data as a datasheet, the datasheet itself didn't contain the summary. That meant you either had to create a report that contained a summary calculation at the end, build a query that totaled the values in one or more fields, or do some quick mental arithmetic. In Access 2007, you can add a Totals row to a datasheet, bypassing the need to create a specific report or query to calculate the total.

Add a Totals Row

① Display a form in Datasheet view.

② Click the Home tab.

③ In the Records group, click Totals.

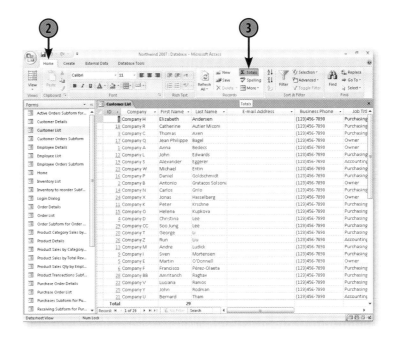

See Also

For more information on viewing a form or report in Datasheet view, see "Working with Database Objects" on page 21.

See Also

For more information on adding a summary calculation to a report, see "Calculating Values in a Report" on page 134.

Adding a Picture

The Chinese philosopher Confucius said that a picture is worth ten thousand words. His wisdom still holds true—a photograph of a product or a diagram of a process can provide valuable contextual information to help you and your colleagues understand form and report data. Also, whether you work for yourself or for a large organization, it's important to add your logo to any documents you want to distribute outside your organization.

Another important consideration when adding a picture to an Access object is whether to embed the picture in the file, which increases the database file's size every time you use the picture, or to link to a single copy of the picture that travels everywhere with the database. If you use the image frequently, or if it's a large file, you should choose to link to the file instead of embedding it.

Embed a Picture

1. Open a form or report in Design view.

2. If necessary, click the Design tab.

3. Click the Image button.

4. Drag on the form or report to define the image's size.

5. Browse for the picture you want to insert, and double-click it.

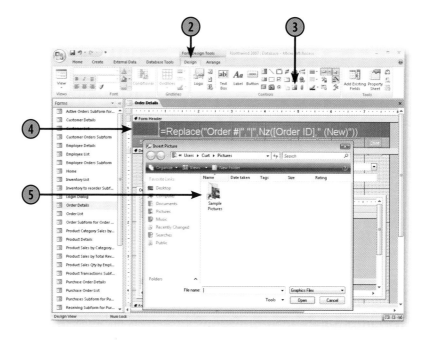

Change an Embedded Picture to a Linked Picture

1. Open the form or report containing the picture in Design view.

2. Click the embedded picture.

3. If necessary, click the Design tab.

4. Click Property Sheet.

5. If necessary, click the Format tab.

6. Click the Picture Type box.

7. Click the down arrow.

8. Click Linked.

9. Click No.

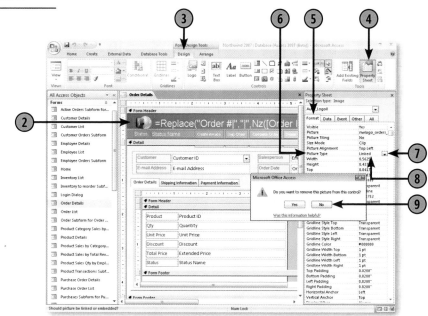

See Also

For more information about adding borders to your pictures, see "Adding Lines, Shapes, and Borders" on page 154.

Applying Conditional Formatting

Changing the appearance of your form and report data by applying formats (or AutoFormats) makes your data easier to read. However, you may want to apply different formats to a control's contents based on the data's value. For example, you might want to highlight the names of any customers who are within 10 percent of their credit limit or display information about discontinued products in red.

Define a Conditional Format

① Open a form or report in Design view.

② Click the control to which you want to apply a conditional format.

③ If necessary, click the Design tab.

④ In the Font group, click Conditional.

⑤ Click the comparison phrase field's down arrow and then click the desired comparison.

⑥ Type values into the value fields to define the condition's parameters.

⑦ Use the Bold, Italic, Underline, Fill Color, Font Color, and Enabled buttons to define the conditional format.

⑧ If desired, follow either of these steps:

- Click Add to define another condition.

- Click Delete, select which conditions you want to delete, and then click OK to delete a condition.

⑨ Click OK.

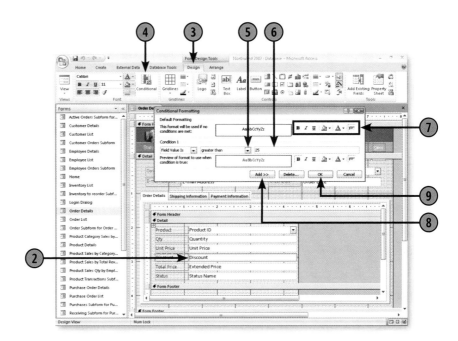

Caution

If you change the appearance of a control's contents by making the contents bold or increasing the font size, be sure the control is large enough to display the data.

Tip

If you create multiple conditions, make sure there is no overlap between the conditions, such as one condition checking whether a number is less than 3000 and another checking whether the same number is less than 1500. If there is overlap, the first condition Access checks is applied. The proper way to create the conditions is to check in Condition 1 if a value is between 1500 and 3000 and then check in Condition 2 if the value is less than 1500.

Changing the Source of an Image

If you work with one organization for a while, you'll probably need to change the images on some of your forms and reports. Whether the change is to update a product's photograph or to change from an old department logo to a new one, you can make the change quickly by identifying the new image in the control's Picture property. The advantage of making the change in the Property Sheet task pane is that you can save time by not deleting and replacing the previous image. Another consideration is that the image is placed in the same control, meaning you won't have to resize the image.

Define a New Image Source

1. Open the form that contains the image in Design view.

2. Click the image you want to change.

3. If necessary, click the Design tab.

4. Click Property Sheet.

5. Click the Format tab.

6. Click Picture.

7. Click the Build button.

8. Click the new target image file.

9. Click Open.

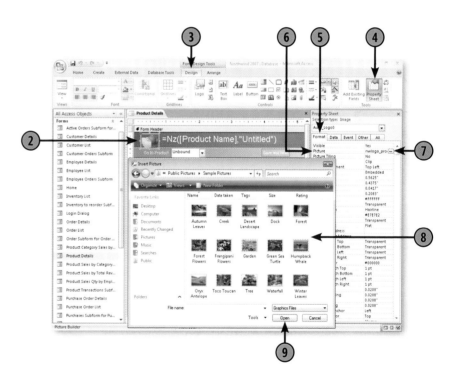

Setting Image Alignment and Backing Color

When you add an image to a form or report, you actually create a control and designate the image as the contents of that control. Because the image is contained within a control, you can use the edges of the control as a frame through which you view the image. As an example, suppose that you have a large image illustrating a process, but the two critical areas you need to show on a form are in opposite corners of the image. By setting the image's alignment within the control, you can align the image so any corner is displayed, meaning you can display the sections of the image you need to show without cropping, editing, or otherwise mangling the image itself. If there is space between the edge of the image and the control's border, you can fill the rest of the control with a background color to provide a frame around the image.

Set a Backing Color

1. Open the form that contains the image in Design view.

2. Click the image you want to change.

3. If necessary, click the Design tab.

4. Click Property Sheet.

5. Click the Format tab.

6. Click Back Color.

7. Click the ellipses arrow.

8. Click the desired color.

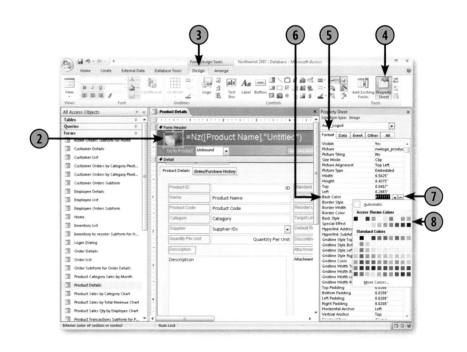

See Also

For more information about formatting the borders of a control, see "Adding Lines, Shapes, and Borders" on page 154.

Change a Picture's Alignment

① Open the form that contains the image in Design view.

② Click the image you want to change.

③ If necessary, click the Design tab.

④ Click Property Sheet.

⑤ Click the Format tab.

⑥ Click Picture Alignment.

⑦ Click the down arrow.

⑧ Click the desired alignment.

Tip

If you want to see the Detail section of the form or any objects behind the image, change the Back Style property's value to Transparent.

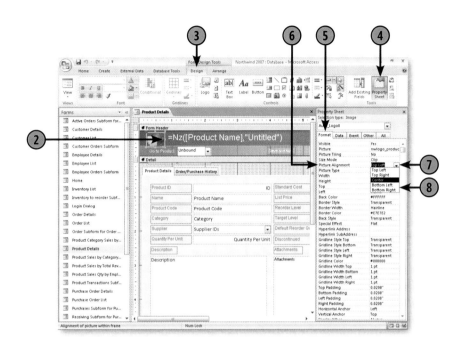

Tiling a Picture

When you add an image to a form or report, you usually want the image to appear in one place. Some images are meant to be repeated, however. For example, you could create a small, square graphic with a repeating pattern, or texture, that you'd like to appear as the background for your form or report. When you repeat an image, you use instances of the image like tiles in a mosaic—the images are placed side by side and cover the entire inside of your image control.

Repeat a Picture on a Form or Report

① Open the form that contains the image in Design view.

② Click the image you want to change.

③ If necessary, click the Design tab.

④ Click Property Sheet.

⑤ Click the Format tab.

⑥ Click Picture Tiling.

⑦ Click the down arrow.

⑧ Click Yes.

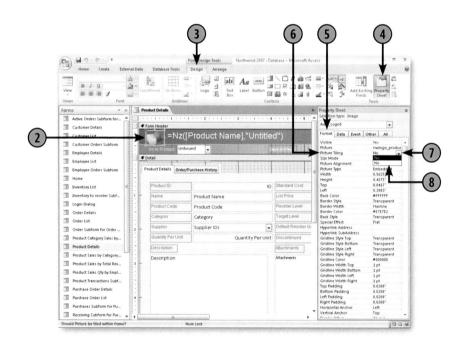

Tip

You can buy textures in most software stores or create your own with a graphics program. The keys to creating a great texture are to make sure you can't see the edges of the individual graphics and to keep the texture file as small as possible.

Setting Image Height and Width

When you design a form or report, you often have the freedom to move things around and make images as large or small as you need to create an attractive design. There are times, however, when space on the page is at a premium and you need to restrict the space an image takes up. You can set the height and width of an image control by setting its Height and Width properties in the Property Sheet task pane.

You can also change how an image will react when you resize its control. If you want, you can have the image stretch to match the new frame size, remain the same size (and possibly have part of the image be hidden), or resize the image to fit within the control while retaining the original height and width ratio.

Set a Precise Image Height and Width

① Open the form that contains the image in Design view.

② Click the image you want to change.

③ If necessary, click the Design tab.

④ Click Property Sheet.

⑤ Click the Format tab.

⑥ Click Size Mode.

⑦ In the Width field, type the desired width.

⑧ In the Height field, type the desired height.

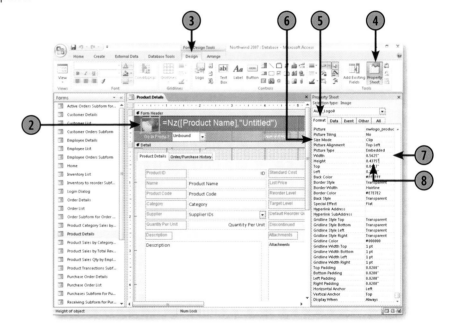

Tip

If you add an image to a form or report and want to ensure all other images you add to other database objects are the same size as that image, write down the values in the Height and Width property boxes.

Set an Image's Resizing Property

① Open the form that contains the image in Design view.

② Click the image you want to change.

③ If necessary, click the Design tab.

④ Click Property Sheet.

⑤ Click the Format tab.

⑥ Click Size Mode.

⑦ Click the down arrow.

⑧ Click the desired size mode.

See Also

For information about changing how an image is aligned within a control, see "Setting Image Alignment and Backing Color" on page 164.

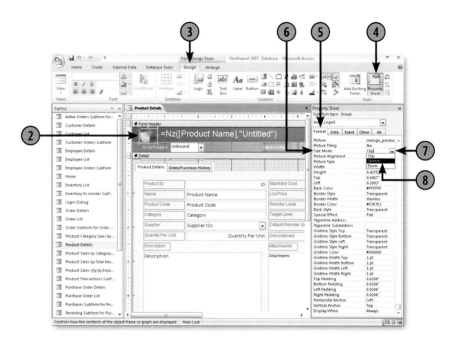

Creating Charts in Access

When you enter data into a Microsoft Office Access database table, you create a record of important events, whether they are individual product sales, sales for an hour of a day, or product prices. What a long list of table values in cells can't communicate easily, however, are the overall trends in the data. The best way to communicate trends in a large collection of data is by creating a chart that summarizes data visually.

You have a great deal of control over your chart's appearance—you can change the color of any chart element, modify a chart's type to better summarize the underlying data, and change the display properties of text and numbers in a chart. What's more, you can add text boxes and legends to provide information that either doesn't appear in the underlying data or is difficult to summarize visually.

Creating a Chart

Access tables store lots of raw data—contact names, sales figures, prices, salaries, and so on. Raw numbers are great for calculations but aren't ideal when you need to describe the data to another human being. Charts and graphs, which summarize data visually, enable you to communicate data values and trends, whether for your own use or for inclusion in a business report.

Build a New Chart

1. Open a blank form in Design view.
2. If necessary, click the Design tab.
3. Click the Insert Chart button.
4. Drag the mouse pointer to define the chart's area.
5. Select the option button to display your database's tables, queries, or both.
6. Click the table or query to provide chart data.
7. Click Next.
8. Click the first field to add to the chart.
9. Click the Add button.
10. Repeat steps 8 and 9 to add more fields to the chart.
11. Click Next.

(continued on the next page)

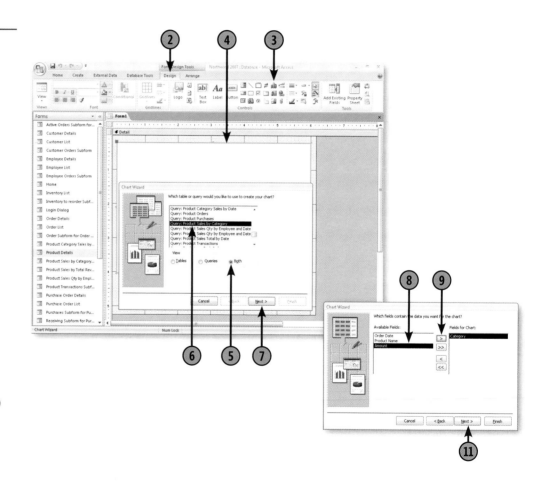

Build a New Chart *(continued)*

⑫ Click the desired chart type.

⑬ Click Next.

⑭ Verify that the chart appears the way you want it to and then click Next.

⑮ Type a name for the chart.

⑯ Select the option button that reflects whether you want to display a legend or not.

⑰ Click Finish.

Tip

You can see what your chart will look like by clicking the Preview Chart button at the top left of the wizard page.

Caution

When you view a form or report with a chart in Design view, the chart might not reflect the data you used to create it. Don't panic! When you switch to Form view for a form (Preview view for a report), the chart will be correct.

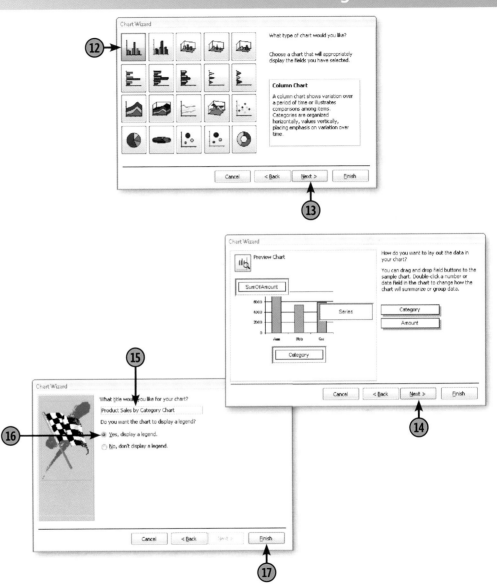

Formatting Chart Elements

Charts present your data visually, so take the time to format your chart elements so it presents your data collection in its best light. Access 2007 lets you change the appearance of any chart element, which means that you can change the chart's appearance to match your corporate color scheme, the data stands out, and the axes and explanatory text complement the data effectively.

Change an Element's Fill Color

1. Open the form in Design view.

2. Double-click the chart.

3. Click the chart element you want to format.

4. On the Formatting toolbar, click the Fill Color button's down arrow.

5. Click the desired color.

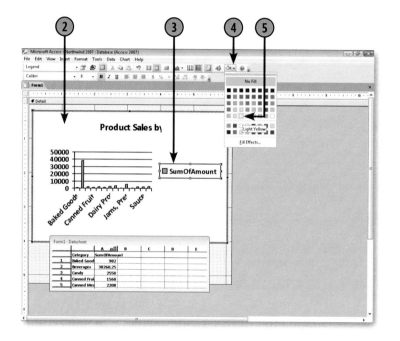

Tip

If you don't see the Fill Color button on the Standard toolbar, hover your mouse pointer over the left edge of the Formatting toolbar, just to the left of the Font control. Drag the Formatting toolbar down until it occupies a second row in the toolbar area.

Change an Element's Font, Size, and Style

1. Open the form in Design view.
2. Double-click the chart.
3. Click the chart element you want to format.
4. Using the controls on the Formatting toolbar, follow any of these steps:
   - Click the Font control's down arrow, and click the desired font.
   - Click the Font Size control's down arrow, and click the desired size.
   - Click the Bold, Italic, or Underline button to apply or remove the style.

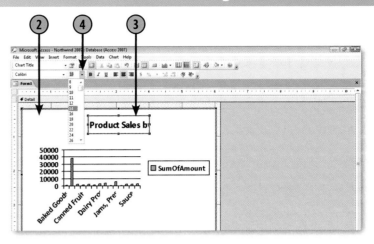

Change an Element's Number Format

1. Open the form in Design view.
2. Double-click the chart.
3. Click the chart element you want to format.
4. Using the controls on the Formatting toolbar, follow these steps:
   - Click the Currency button to apply the Accounting number format.
   - Click the Percent Style button to display the number as a percentage.
   - Click the Comma Style button to display the number using commas as a thousands separator.
   - Click the Increase Decimal or Decrease Decimal button to add or remove decimal places from the number.

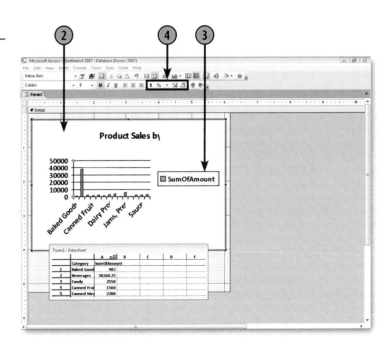

Customizing Chart Axes

Access charts summarize numerical data, such as sales figures, project labor costs, class attendance, grades, and donations received. Typically, you are able to divide your data into a set of categories, such as product types, projects, or months. The structure of the table or query that provides data for your chart determines how your chart appears, but you can decide whether to add a title to identify the types of values displayed on the horizontal or vertical axis. You can also make it easier to compare values on your chart by displaying or hiding the gridlines that mark values on the vertical axis and categories on the horizontal axis.

Add a Title to an Axis

① Open the form in Design view.

② Double-click the chart.

③ On the menu bar, click Chart.

④ Click Chart Options.

⑤ If necessary, click the Titles tab.

⑥ Follow either or both of these steps:

  ■ Type a title for the horizontal axis in the Category (X) Axis box.

  ■ Type a title for the vertical axis in the Value (Y) Axis box.

⑦ Click OK.

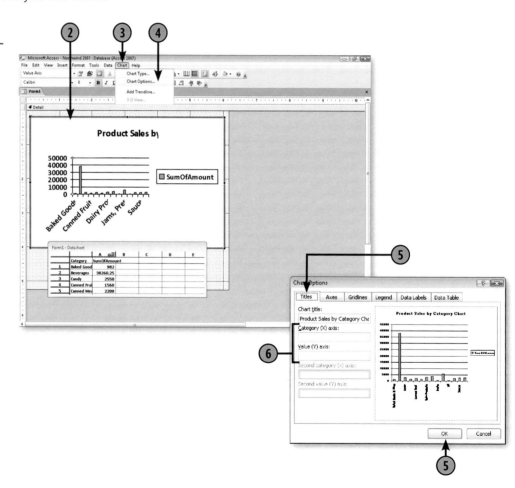

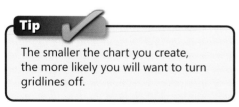

Tip

The smaller the chart you create, the more likely you will want to turn gridlines off.

Show or Hide Axis Gridlines

① Open the form in Design view.

② Double-click the chart.

③ Using the controls on the Standard toolbar, follow either of these steps:

- ■ Click the Category Axis Gridlines button to show or hide the horizontal axis's gridlines.

- ■ Click the Value Axis Gridlines button to show or hide the vertical axis's gridlines.

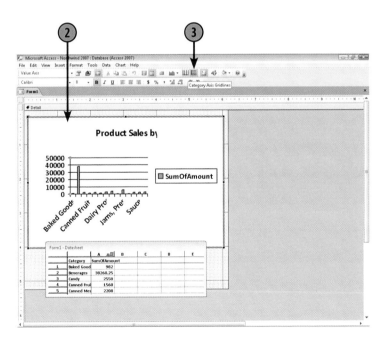

Add Information to a Chart

As much as you might like to think your Access chart data is self-explanatory, adding contextual information to your chart's form helps your audience understand the chart's data. A legend, which lists both the data series displayed in a chart and the colors used to represent the series, allows chart viewers to associate the chart's contents with your organization's results. You can also add text boxes that contain explanatory text to emphasize specific aspects of your data or to provide information not easily communicated in a chart.

Show or Hide a Chart Legend

① Open the form in Design view.

② Double-click the chart.

③ On the Standard toolbar, click the Legend button.

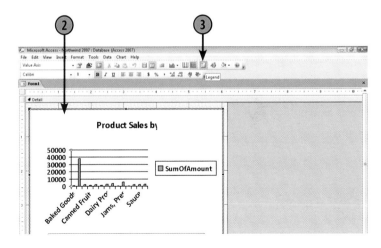

Change the Legend's Location

① Open the form in Design view.

② Double-click the chart.

③ On the menu bar, click Chart.

④ Click Chart Options.

⑤ If necessary, click the Legend tab.

⑥ Select the Placement option that represents where you want the legend to appear.

⑦ Click OK.

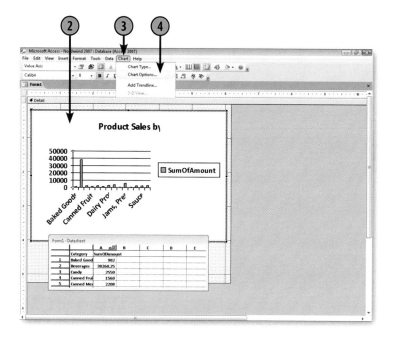

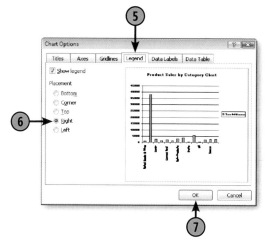

Add a Text Box

1. Open the form in Design view.

2. Double-click the chart.

3. On the Standard toolbar, click the Drawing button.

4. Click the Text Box button.

5. Drag the mouse pointer to define the text box.

6. Type the text to appear in the text box.

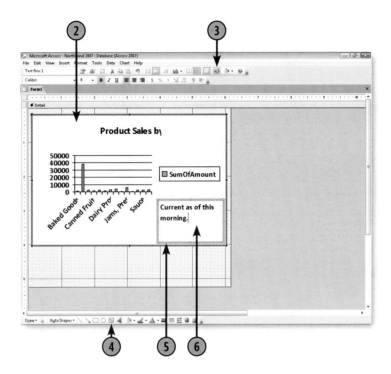

Changing a Chart's Type

Organizations store data of all kinds: stock reports, sales figures, department profits, information technology expenditures, and so on. Different data types demand different presentations, so you need to select the most appropriate chart type for your data. Access 2007 enables you to create 18 different types of charts, so you can experiment with your form to discover the chart type that summarizes your data most effectively.

Select a Different Chart Type

① Open the form in Design view.

② Double-click the chart.

③ On the Standard toolbar, click the Chart Type button's down arrow.

④ Click the desired chart type.

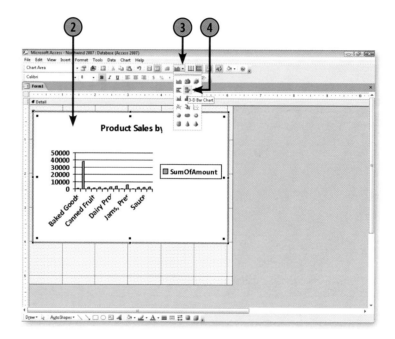

13

Interacting with Other Programs

Microsoft Office Access 2007 is a powerful program, but it doesn't try to do everything. Other programs in the Microsoft Office 2007 suite have complementary strengths: Word is great for creating text documents, Excel is ideal for recording and analyzing financial information, and PowerPoint lets you convert your thoughts into attractive presentations you can print out or project onto a screen for audiences of hundreds or even thousands. You can also add images you create in a graphics program or capture with a scanner or digital camera.

Access also gives you a lot of versatility in interacting with other companies or individuals who might not keep their databases in Access. You can easily export your Access table data and query results into lots of other file formats or bring in data from the same programs.

Introducing Linking and Embedding

Access works wonderfully as a stand-alone program, but it really shines when you use it in combination with other programs. One way to use Access in conjunction with other programs is to include files created in other programs, such as graphics, text documents created in Word, PowerPoint presentations, or Excel charts and worksheets in your forms and reports. You can add these objects to your database through linking and embedding.

Linking and embedding are done through the same dialog box, but there are several important things you need to keep in mind when you decide whether to link to an object or to embed it in a form or report. As the name implies, embedding an object in a form or report stores a copy of the object with the database. For example, if you want to add a company logo to an invoice generated from table data, you could identify the graphic and indicate you want to embed it in the database. The advantage of embedding an object in a database is that you never have to worry about the graphic, chart, or spreadsheet not being available because the person pulling up the form or report has copied the database to a computer without the embedded file. If you create databases with embedded files, you can travel anywhere, secure in the knowledge that the files will be there.

The downside to embedding objects in databases is that the embedded files can be quite large and increase the size of the database file significantly. While a single, low-resolution logo meant to be viewed on a computer monitor probably won't have much of an impact on your file size, the same image rendered at a resolution suitable for printing might double the size of the database. If you embed more than one image or more than one copy of the same image, you might make your database unworkably large.

When you want to include more than one image or external file in an Access database, the best choice may be to create a link to the files in the form or report. For example, rather than embed many copies of a high-resolution logo in your reports, you could save the file on your computer and link to the file's location on your computer. Access uses the reference to find the file and display it as part of a database object. The database is no larger than it was originally, and you don't need to have multiple copies of the same document if you link to it more than once. So, the advantage of linking is that you save hard drive space, but the disadvantage is that moving from computer to computer can be difficult unless you take the non-Access files with you when you travel. In general, embed an object in an Access database if you use the object once and you have room to store the database (with the only included object) when you travel. In other cases, such as when you use the same file multiple times in the same database, consider linking to the file and not embedding it.

Inserting a New Object

Access tables and queries hold a lot of data, but you can augment your Access data with information in files created with other programs. For example, you might create a Word document with important background information or a PowerPoint presentation that puts your data into context for your colleagues. You can include those files in your Access forms and reports by linking or embedding the files as objects.

Embed an Existing Object

① Open a form or report in Design view.

② Click the Design tab.

③ Click the Unbound Object Frame button.

④ Drag on the body of the form to define the frame's boundaries.

⑤ Select the Create from File option.

⑥ Click Browse.

(continued on the next page)

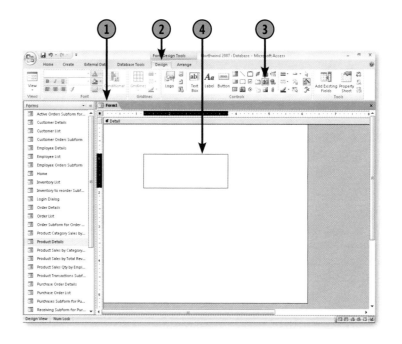

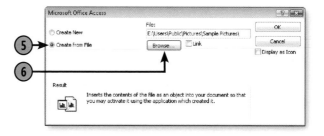

Embed an Existing Object *(continued)*

⑦ Navigate to the folder that contains the target file.

⑧ Click the target file.

⑨ Click OK to close the Browse dialog box.

⑩ Click OK to close the Microsoft Office Access dialog box.

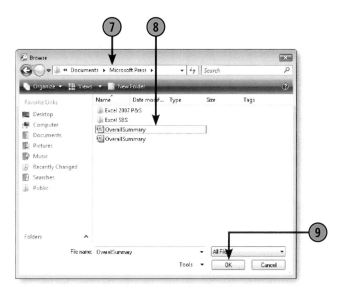

Link to an Existing Object

1. Open a form or report in Design view.

2. Click the Design tab.

3. Click the Unbound Object Frame button.

4. Drag on the body of the form to define the frame's boundaries.

5. Select the Create from File option.

6. Click Browse.

7. Navigate to the folder that contains the target file.

8. Click the target file.

9. Click OK to close the Browse dialog box.

10. Select the Link check box.

11. Click OK to close the Microsoft Office Access dialog box.

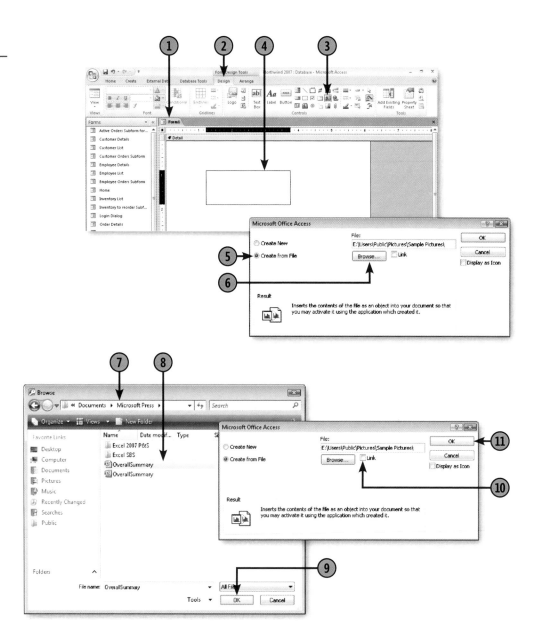

Tip

If you want to link or embed an object but don't want it to take up much space on the form or report, select the Display as Icon check box to display the file's Windows icon instead of the object itself.

Manipulating Objects

Once you add an object to a form or report, you can work with it in the same way you work with form or report controls. For example, if you want to display the same image at the top and bottom of a report, you could do so by adding the image

to the report, copying it, and then pasting it at the bottom of the report. If the object you created isn't in the right position or isn't the correct size, you can move or resize it so that it fits into your form or report in exactly the right way.

Copy an Object

① Display a form or report in Design view.

② Click the object you want to copy.

③ Click the Home tab.

④ Click the Copy button.

Paste an Object

① Display a form or report in Design view.

② Click the Home tab.

③ Click the Paste button.

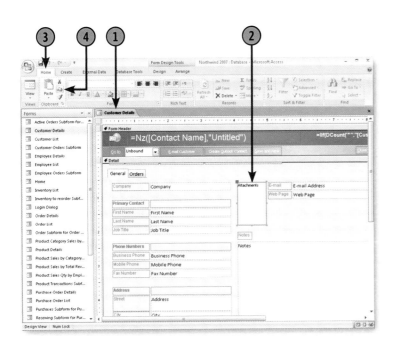

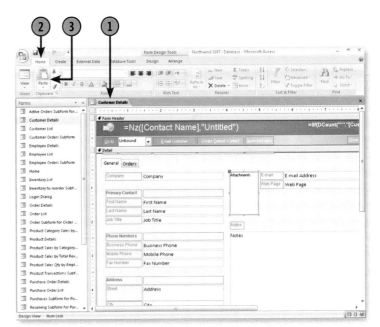

Move an Object

① Display a form or report in Design view.

② Drag an object to its new location.

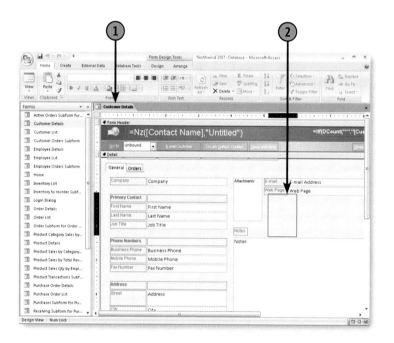

Resize an Object

(1) Display a form or report in Design view.

(2) Click the object you want to resize.

(3) Position the mouse pointer over an edge or corner of the object.

(4) Drag the edge or corner until the object is the desired size.

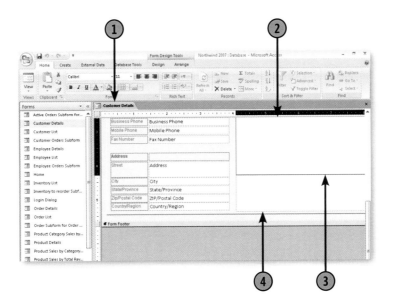

See Also

For more information about rearranging your objects on a form or report, see "Setting Control Appearance" on page 149.

Inserting Excel Charts and Worksheets

Access is designed to let you store, manipulate, and ask questions of large amounts of data. Excel offers a wide range of data analysis and presentation tools you can use to extend the analysis you perform in Access. Including an Excel chart or worksheet in an Access form or report lets you explore alternative scenarios, use past data to project future patterns, or summarize your data in ways not available in Access summary queries.

Add an Excel Chart

① Open a form or report in Design view.

② Click the Design tab.

③ Click the Unbound Object Frame button.

④ Drag on the body of the form to define the frame's boundaries.

⑤ If necessary, select the Create New option.

⑥ Click the Microsoft Office Excel Chart object type.

⑦ Click OK.

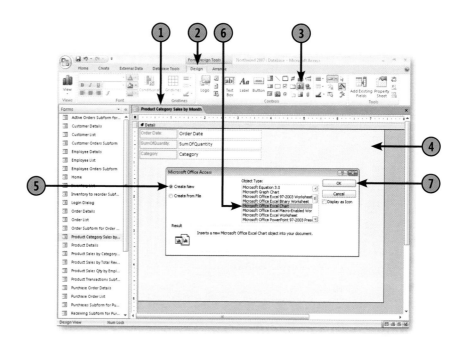

Tip

The Excel Chart control is an Excel workbook that contains a worksheet and a chart sheet. To change the data displayed in the chart, click the Sheet1 worksheet tab and edit the data there.

Add an Excel Worksheet

1. Open a form or report in Design view.

2. Click the Design tab.

3. Click the Unbound Object Frame button.

4. Drag on the body of the form to define the frame's boundaries.

5. If necessary, select the Create New option.

6. Click the Microsoft Office Excel Worksheet object type.

7. Click OK.

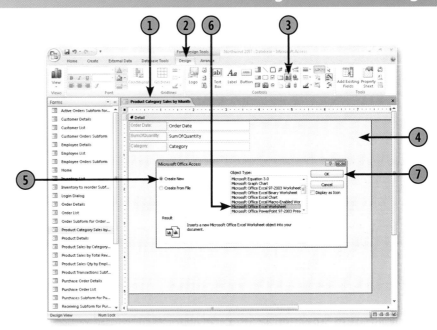

Importing Data from Another Access Database

One way to think of an Access database is as a collection of facts about a particular subject. For example, you could have a database that tracks your sales contacts and correspondence, another database that tracks your product inventory, and yet another that tracks your vehicles and the miles they drive. It makes sense to separate your data into topic-based databases, but there are times when a table from one database is useful in another database. For example, if you want to use data from a table in a database that's hosted on another computer, consider importing that data into your own database to guard against the network being down or the database being unavailable. Access 2007 also lets you save the import operation so you can repeat the steps quickly the next time you want to import the same table or tables.

Import One or More Tables

(1) Click the External Data tab.

(2) In the Import group, click Access.

(3) Select the Import Tables, Queries, Forms, Reports, Macros, And Modules Into The Current Database option.

(4) Click Browse.

(5) Navigate to the folder that contains the database from which you want to import a table.

(6) Double-click the database.

(7) Click OK.

(continued on the next page)

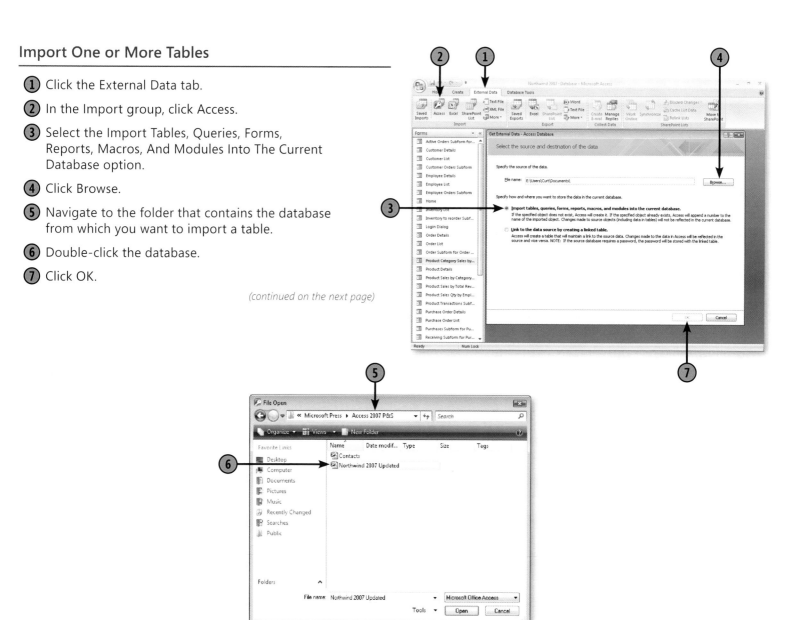

Import One or More Tables *(continued)*

8 Click the Tables tab.

9 Click the tables you want to import.

10 Click OK.

11 Select the Save Import Steps check box.

12 Type a name for the import operation.

13 If desired, type a description for the import operation.

14 Click Save Import.

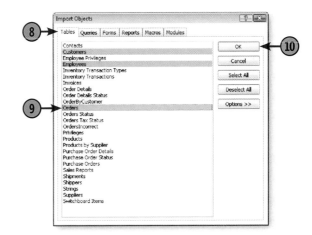

Caution

Importing a table from another database means you don't have to type the data a second time, but you must be sure either that the copied table's contents won't change or that it doesn't matter if the table's contents do change. If the table's contents change regularly, the absolute worst thing you can do is create a second version of the same table. For example, if you start tracking sales contacts in two databases, everyone needs to know that the separate tables exist and where to find them. Not only would they have to enter the data twice, there would be twice as many opportunities for data entry errors.

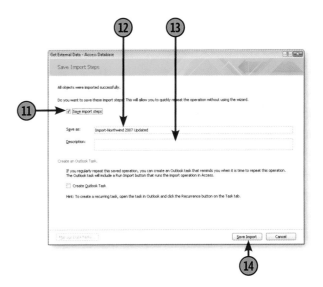

See Also

For information on linking to a table in another database, see "Linking to a Table in Another Access Database" on page 192.

Linking to a Table in Another Access Database

When you first start using Access, it can be tempting to store all of your data about everything in a single database. The names and addresses of sales contacts could live beside the list of product categories, but they really shouldn't. It's better to create separate databases to store data on specific subjects, such as products or sales leads. If you do need to use data from one database in another database, you can do so. For example, if you track active customers in your orders database, you can use the same table in your sales contacts database. Access enables you to create links to tables in other databases. Linking to another table means that every change made to the table in the original database, or in the database with the link, appears in the table. Unlike when you copy a table from one database to another, linking ensures that the data is available to everyone who needs it.

Create a Link to a Table

① Click the External Data tab.

② In the Import group, click Access.

③ Select the Link To The Data Source By Creating A Linked Table option.

④ Click Browse.

⑤ Navigate to the folder that contains the target database.

⑥ Double-click the target database.

⑦ Click OK.

(continued on the next page)

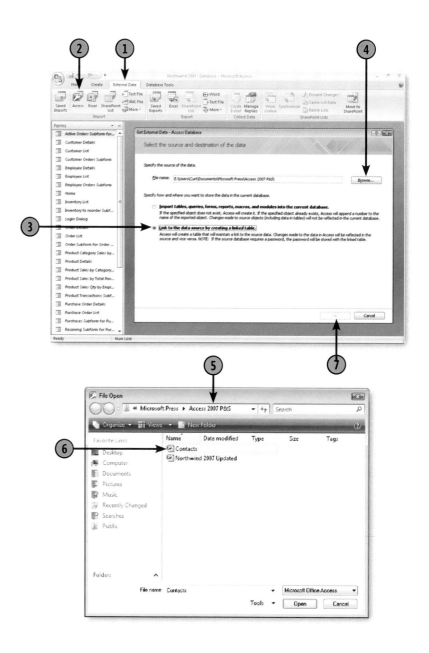

Create a Link to a Table *(continued)*

8 Click the tables to which you want to create a link.

9 Click OK.

Access displays the linked table with all of your database's other tables, but the linked table's icon has a right-pointing arrow at its top-left corner, indicating that it's a linked table.

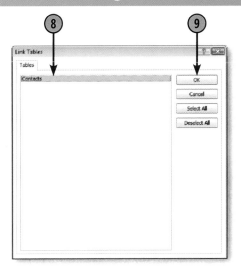

Working with Hyperlinks

A fundamental characteristic of the World Wide Web is the ability to create connections—called *hyperlinks*—between related documents. By creating hyperlinks to helpful files on the Web, or even to objects in the current Access database, you can provide useful information to anyone viewing the page. Those documents may in turn have links that lead you away from the main document. You can easily return to the database page quickly by clicking your Web browser's Back button or, if a hyperlink leads to a Web page viewed in a Web browser, you can simply switch back to the Access window. Hyperlinks to Web pages start with http://, but a hyperlink to a file in the same directory as the database consists of just the file's name. If the file name occurs in a field with the Hyperlink data type, Access knows to display the file name as a hyperlink.

Create a Hyperlink to
an Existing File

① Display a form or report in Design view.

② Click the Design tab.

③ Click the Hyperlink button.

④ Click Existing File Or Web Page.

⑤ Click the Browse For File button.

⑥ Navigate to the folder that contains the file to which you want to link.

⑦ Double-click the file to which you want to link.

⑧ Type a short phrase to describe the hyperlink's target.

⑨ Click OK.

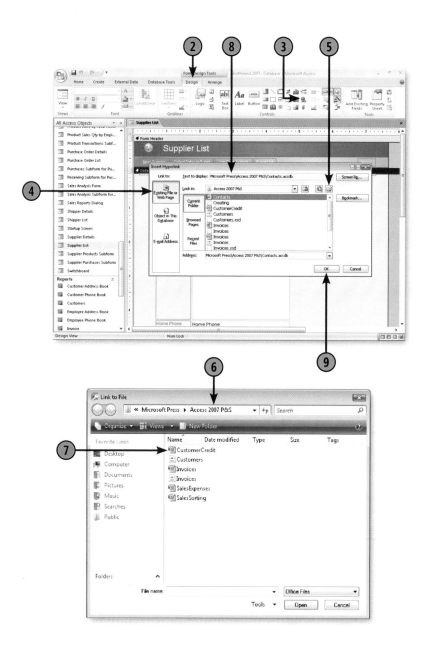

Create a Hyperlink to a Web Page

1. Display a form or report in Design view.
2. Click the Design tab.
3. Click the Hyperlink button.
4. Click Browsed Pages.
5. Click the page to which you want to link.
6. Type a short phrase to describe the hyperlink's target.
7. Click OK.

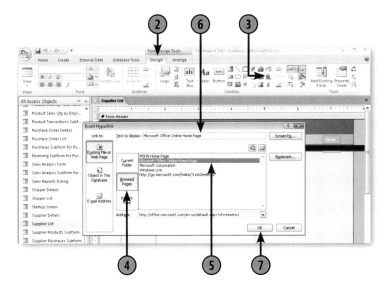

Create a Hyperlink to an Existing Database Object

1. Display a form or report in Design view.
2. Click the Design tab.
3. Click the Hyperlink button.
4. Click Object In This Database.
5. Click the show detail control next to the desired object type.
6. Click the database object to which you want to link.
7. Type a short phrase to describe the hyperlink's target.
8. Click OK.

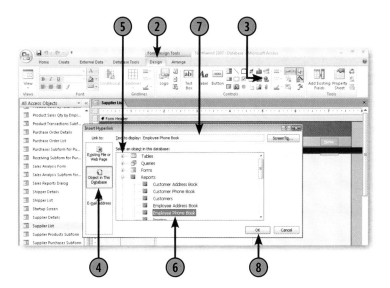

Tip

If you know the URL of the Web page to which you want to link, you can type it directly into the Address box of the Insert Hyperlink dialog box.

Importing Data from an Excel File

On the surface, Excel and Access look a lot alike. Both programs handle data lists effectively. In fact, some small-business owners maintain all of their data lists in Excel and use that program's summary functions, sorting, and filtering capabilities as if Excel were a database program. That's fine if you have a single data table you want to analyze, but there's no easy way to create relationships between tables, define queries using filters, or generate reports. Fortunately, there's a straightforward process you can follow to bring an Excel data list into Access. Once your Excel data is in a database, you can create reports and queries that are possible, but very hard, to create in Excel.

Import Excel Data

(1) Click the External Data tab.

(2) In the Import group, click Excel.

(3) Select the Import The Source Data Into A New Table In The Current Database option.

(4) Click Browse.

(5) Navigate to the folder that contains the desired Excel file.

(6) Double-click the file.

(7) Click OK.

(continued on the next page)

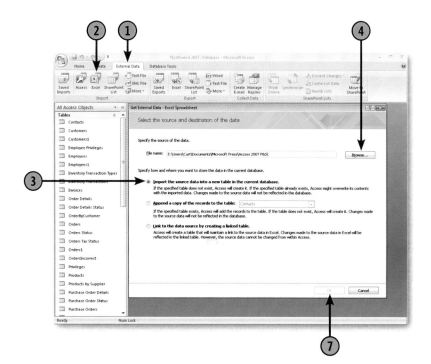

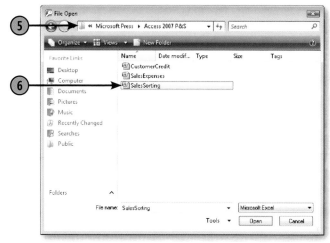

Import Excel Data *(continued)*

⑧ Click the type of data sources you want to display.

⑨ Click the specific source from which you want to draw your data.

⑩ Click Next.

⑪ If the first row of the Excel table contains the desired column headings, select the First Row Contains Column Headings check box.

⑫ Verify that the data appears to be arranged correctly and click Next.

⑬ Click the data column you want to edit.

⑭ Type a new name for the field.

⑮ Click the Indexed box's down arrow, and select whether you want the field to be indexed and whether to allow duplicate values.

⑯ Click the Data Type box's down arrow, and select the field's data type.

⑰ If necessary, repeat steps 13 through 16 for other fields you want to edit.

⑱ Click Next.

(continued on the next page)

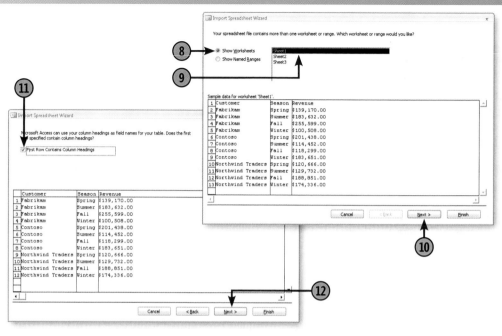

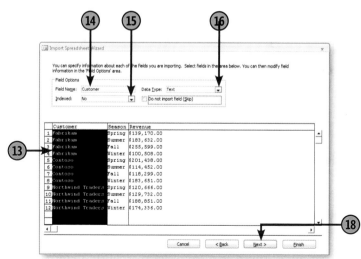

Import Excel Data *(continued)*

⑲ Select the option that indicates how you want Access to assign a primary key to the table.

⑳ If necessary, select the Choose My Own Primary Key option box's down arrow and click the field to use as a primary key.

㉑ Click Next.

㉒ Type a name for the new table.

㉓ Click Finish.

> **Tip** ✓
>
> If you don't want to import a field, display the Field Options page of the Import Spreadsheet Wizard, click the target field, and select the Do Not Import Field (Skip) check box.

> **Caution** !
>
> If the Excel workbook from which you want to copy data contains a single worksheet and no tables or named data ranges, you won't see the wizard page that asks you to identify the data source.

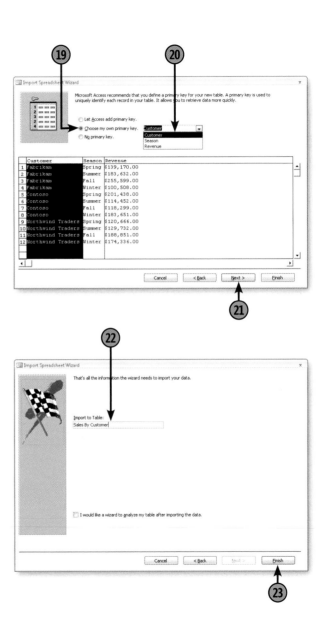

Importing Data from a Text File

In the early days of personal computing, it was very hard to transfer data between programs and, in some cases, between computers. Different computers used different types of disks, programs created files that no other programs could read, and organizations developed solutions that didn't enable information workers to collaborate effectively. However, most programs knew how to deal with data stored as a text file. That's still the case today. If you absolutely must work with data from a program that can't create another data format Access understands, you can always have your colleagues export their data as a text file. Access knows how to convert text files to database tables, which then enables you to integrate the new data into your database.

Import Text Data

1. Click the External Data tab.

2. In the Import group, click Text File.

3. Select the Import The Source Data Into A New Table In The Current Database option.

4. Click Browse.

5. Navigate to the folder that contains the desired text file.

6. Double-click the file.

7. Click OK.

(continued on the next page)

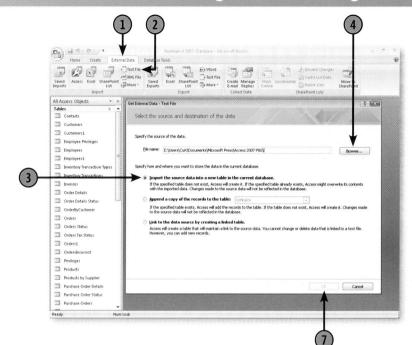

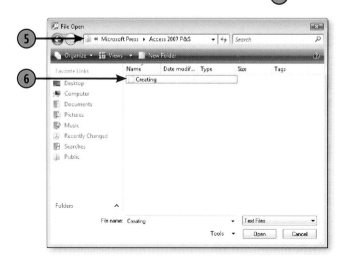

Import Text Data *(continued)*

8 Select the option button that reflects whether the source file's data contains field delimiters or whether the fields contain fixed numbers of characters.

9 Click Next.

10 Select the option that reflects the delimiter character.

11 If necessary, select the First Row Contains Field Names check box.

12 Click Next.

(continued on the next page)

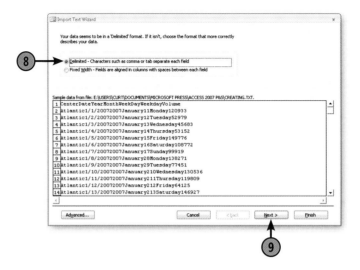

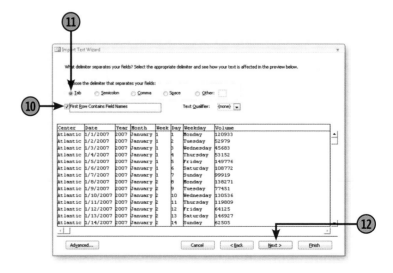

Import Text Data (continued)

⑬ Click the data column you want to edit.

⑭ Type a new name for the field.

⑮ Click the Indexed box's down arrow and select whether you want the field to be indexed and whether to allow duplicate values.

⑯ Click the Data Type box's down arrow, and select the field's data type.

⑰ If necessary, repeat steps 13 through 16 for other fields you want to edit.

⑱ Click Next.

⑲ Select the option button that indicates how you want Access to assign a primary key to the table.

⑳ Click Next.

㉑ Type a name for the new table.

㉒ Click Finish.

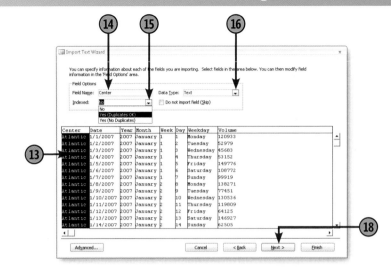

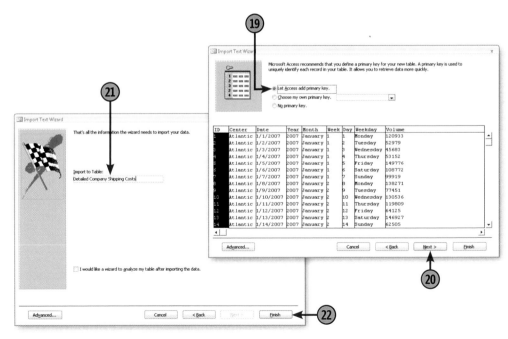

Importing Data from an XML File

It's easy to find data analysis programs such as Access and Excel that know how to read data from text files into their native formats. Text files have a couple of important limitations, though. The first limitation is that the files don't contain any formatting details, so any conditional formats, cell colors, or text formatting is lost when you import the data into Access. Similarly, text files don't contain any information describing the data in the file. Sure, you can create a text file that has information about the file's data, who created it, and so on, but Access either imports the data into the table and forces you to delete the nonsense rows, or you have to strip the data from the file before importing the data.

Some really bright folks combined the flexibility of text files with a scheme to include information about a file's contents within the file. The Extensible Markup Language (XML) enables you to save a database table as a text file that contains elements, called tags, that describe the file's contents. What's great about the XML format is that if Access finds a tag it doesn't understand, it ignores it and keeps on importing the file's data.

Import XML Data

1. Click the External Data tab.

2. In the Import group, click XML File.

3. Click Browse.

4. Navigate to the folder that contains the desired XML file.

5. Double-click the file.

6. Click OK.

(continued on the next page)

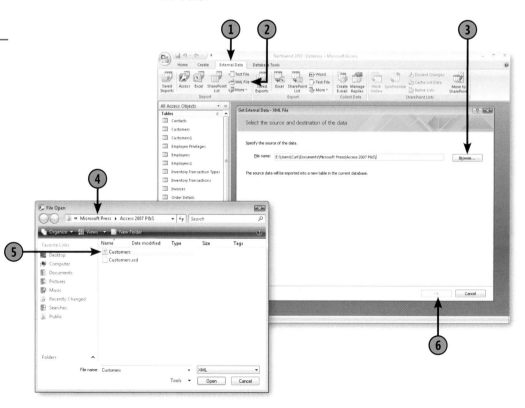

Import XML Data *(continued)*

(7) Click the table that contains the data you want to import.

(8) Click OK.

(9) Select the Save Import Steps option.

(10) Type a name for the saved import operation.

(11) If desired, type a description for the saved import operation.

(12) Click Save Import.

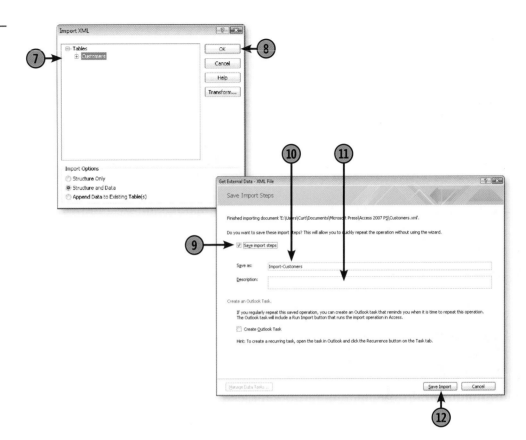

Exporting Data to a Text File

At the most basic level, database tables are collections of text. Company names? Text. Order identifiers? Text. Sales amounts? Text. Yes, you can attach nontextual files such as images to Access 2007 database records, but the directions to those files' locations on your computer or network can always be expressed using text. Most programs know how to process files stored as text, so if you need to interact with a colleague or vendor who's using an older database system or custom application that doesn't interact well (or at all) with Access, export your table or query to a text file and let him or her work with your data in the most universal form available.

Export Text Data

① Click the table you want to export.

② Click the External Data tab.

③ In the Export group, click Text File.

④ Click Browse.

⑤ Navigate to the folder where you want to save the text file.

⑥ Type a name for the file.

⑦ Click Save.

⑧ Click OK.

(continued on the next page)

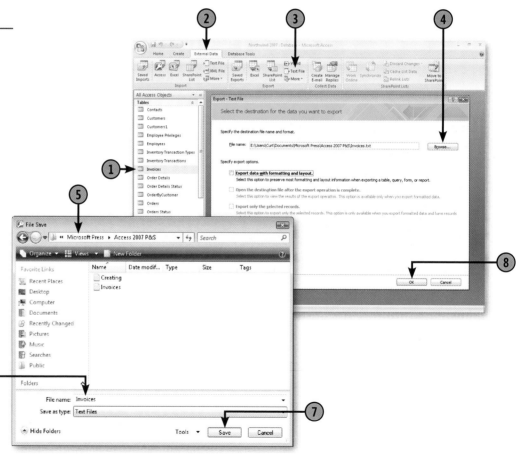

Export Text Data (continued)

⑨ Select the Delimited option.

⑩ Click Next.

⑪ Select the option that represents the delimiter character you want to separate the fields.

⑫ Select the Include Field Names on First Row check box.

⑬ Click Finish.

⑭ Select the Save Export Steps option.

⑮ Type a name for the saved export operation.

⑯ If desired, type a description for the saved export operation.

⑰ Click Save Export.

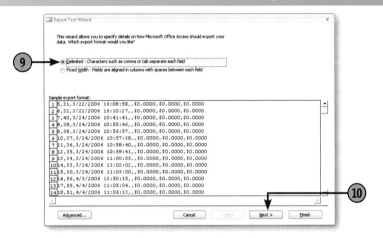

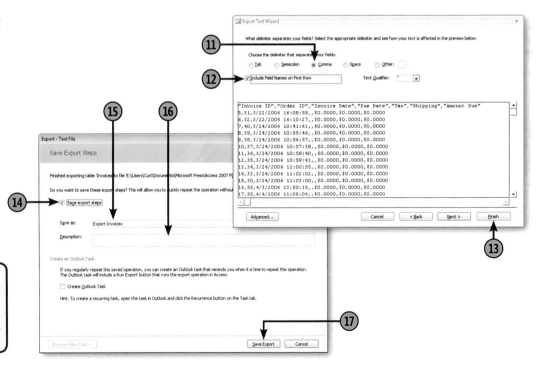

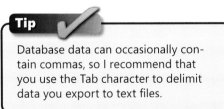

> **Tip** ✓
>
> Database data can occasionally contain commas, so I recommend that you use the Tab character to delimit data you export to text files.

Exporting Data to Another Access File

Dropping all of your paper-based reports, articles, and research into a single file folder doesn't make much sense. Gathering absolutely all of your information into one place is better than throwing it away, but it's only a marginal improvement. Instead, it makes more sense to group your organization's data into distinct databases that each focus on a particular subject. If you are a school administrator, you can use Access to track your students' attendance. Businesses can manage employees' time cards, sales contacts, and the company's product inventory in Access, but it makes sense to create a separate database for each function. If you need to use data from one Access database in another database, you can transfer your data table without any trouble.

Export to Another Access Database

① Click the object you want to export to another database.

② Click the External Data tab.

③ In the Export group, click More.

④ Click Access Database.

(continued on the next page)

 **Tip**

If you type the name of an object that already exists in the target database, Access offers you the choice of replacing the existing object or typing a new name for the object you're exporting.

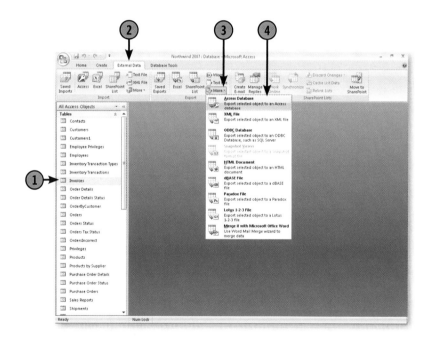

Export to Another
Access Database (continued)

⑤ Click Browse.

⑥ Navigate to the folder with the target database.

⑦ Type the name of the database.

⑧ Click Save.

⑨ Click OK.

⑩ Type a name for the object.

⑪ Click OK.

⑫ Select the Save Export Steps option.

⑬ Type a name for the saved export.

⑭ If desired, type a description for the export.

⑮ Click Save Export.

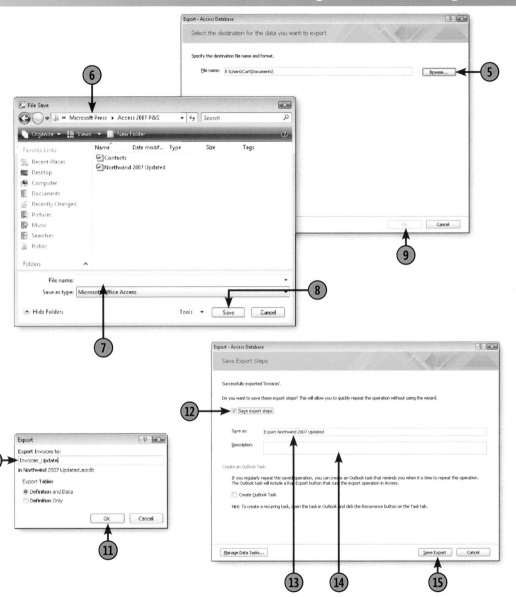

Exporting Data to an XML File

Most programs are able to make use of data stored in text files, but plain text files don't let you store formatting information, data validation rules, or whether a field only allows users to append data to existing values. However, XML provides the means to encode that information into the body of a text file using tags. These tags indicate where a table row begins, where each cell begins and ends, each column's data type, any data validation rules applied to the column, and so on. The files Access creates contain a lot of information that is specific to Access, but because Access creates files with tags most other programs can process, the information about your file usually translates between programs just fine.

Export XML Data

1. Click the object you want to export to another database.
2. Click the External Data tab.
3. In the Export group, click More.
4. Click XML File.

(continued on the next page)

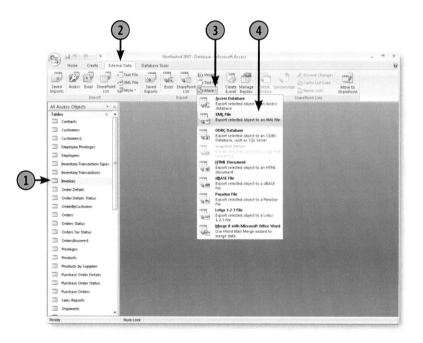

Export XML Data *(continued)*

(5) Click Browse.

(6) Navigate to the folder where you want to save the data file.

(7) Type the file name.

(8) Click Save.

(9) Click OK.

(10) Verify that the Data (XML) and Schema Of The Data (XSD) check boxes are selected.

(11) Click OK.

(12) Select the Save Export Steps option.

(13) Type a name for the saved export.

(14) If desired, type a description for the export.

(15) Click Save Export.

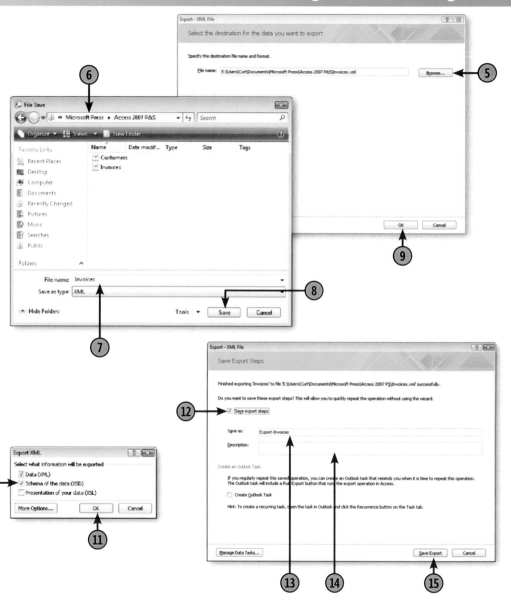

Saving Database Objects as Web Files

One of the easiest ways to communicate data to traveling colleagues is to make that data available on a Web page. Writing the data to a Web page means you don't have to send the entire database file to the traveler. In fact, your colleague doesn't even need Access on his or her machine! Saving database objects as Web pages is also a great way to make data available over a corporate network (an intranet). So long as your company's network supports Web connections, you can make your data available to any authorized user.

Save an Object as a Web File

1 Click the object you want to save as a Web file.

2 Click the External Data tab.

3 In the Export group, click More.

4 Click HTML Document.

(continued on the next page)

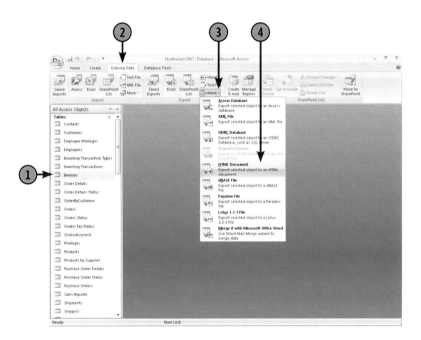

Save an Object as a
Web File *(continued)*

(5) Click Browse.

(6) Navigate to the folder where you want to store the Web file.

(7) If desired, type a new name for the file.

(8) Click Save.

(9) Click OK to close the Export-HTML Document dialog box.

(10) If it appears, click OK to close the HTML Output Options dialog box.

(11) Select the Save Export Steps check box.

(12) Type a name for the saved export.

(13) If desired, type a description for the saved export.

(14) Click Save Export.

Tip

The HTML Output Options dialog box appears when you save a Form or Report. Those objects have Office Themes applied to them; the HTML Output Options dialog box contains tools you can use to select the output options, including changing the Web file's theme.

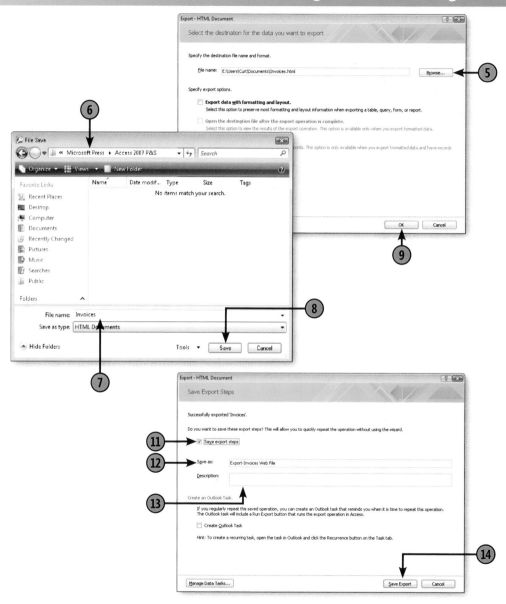

Analyzing Data with Microsoft Excel

Each of the programs in the Microsoft Office 2007 suite has its particular strengths, but Excel and Access have a lot of similarities. Both programs handle data lists well, but where Excel shines at summarizing data using an incredible variety of calculations and formulas, Access enables you to create powerful queries to draw exactly the data you need from your tables.

If you have a table or query that contains exactly the data you want to analyze and summarize in Excel, using summary functions and operations not readily available in Access, step through the following procedure to bring the power of Excel to bear on your data.

Analyze Data in Excel

1. Click the table or query you want to analyze.

2. Click the External Data tab.

3. In the Export group, click the Export to Excel Spreadsheet button.

4. Click Browse.

5. Navigate to the folder where you want to create the Excel workbook.

6. Type a name for the file.

7. Click Save.

(continued on the next page)

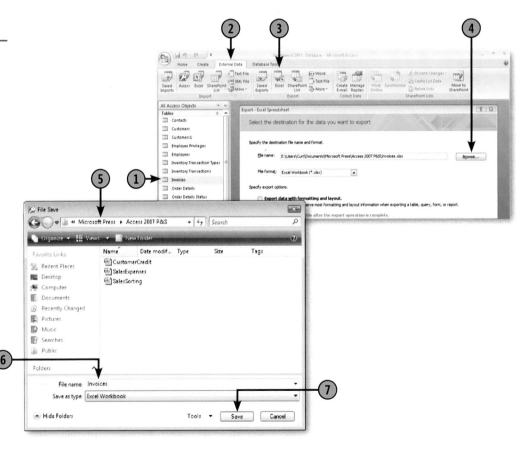

Analyze Data in Excel *(continued)*

8 If desired, select the Export Data With Formatting And Layout option.

9 Click OK.

10 Select the Save Export Steps option.

11 Type a name for the saved export.

12 If desired, type a description for the export.

13 Click Save Export.

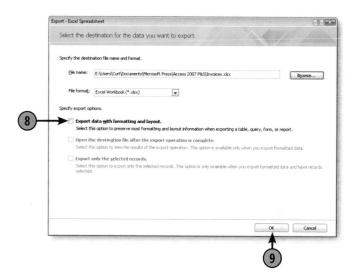

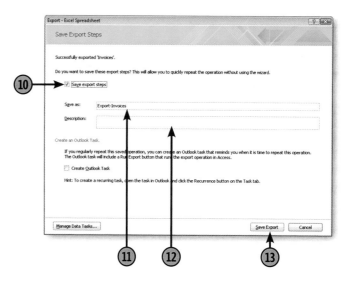

Publishing Data to Microsoft Word

You've probably used Microsoft Word to create documents in your office or at home. Word is great for general correspondence, creating mass mailings, and designing attractive newsletters, but it's not the program you want to use to store large data lists. Yes, you can store data in Word tables, but it's hard to do more than the most rudimentary summaries of that data. Access makes it much easier for you to summarize and find subsets of your data. Then, whether your data is destined to be included in an annual report, a briefing to your boss, or a letter documenting all open invoices with a specific vendor, Access enables you to transfer your data to a Word document efficiently.

Export Data to Word

1. Click the table or query you want to export.

2. Click the External Data tab.

3. In the Export group, click the Word button.

4. Click Browse.

5. Navigate to the folder where you want to create the Word document.

6. Type a name for the file.

7. Click Save.

(continued on the next page)

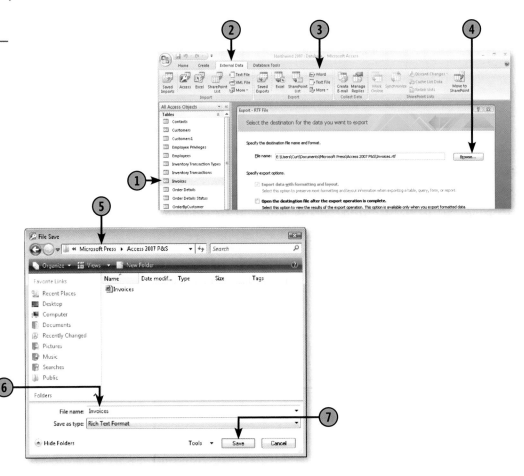

Export Data to Word (continued)

(8) If desired, select the Open The Destination File After The Export Operation Is Complete option.

(9) Click OK.

(10) Select the Save Export Steps option.

(11) Type a name for the saved export.

(12) If desired, type a description for the export.

(13) Click Save Export.

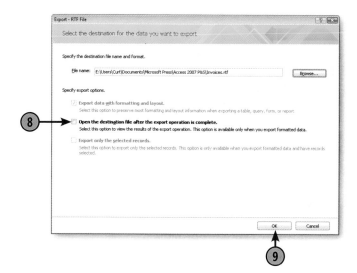

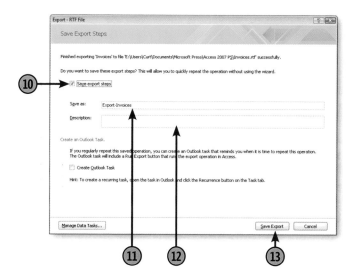

Collecting Data from E-mail Messages

Gathering data from one's colleagues, vendors, and customers can be a frustrating process. When you ask a question by phone, in person, or over e-mail, you end up transcribing the responses and typing them into your database. The potential for inaccuracies, mistranscriptions, and other mistakes abound. One of the most useful new things you can do in Access 2007 is to create Outlook 2007 messages that contain Access forms. You send the form to a colleague as an e-mail message, which the recipient fills out and sends back. You can then read the data directly from Outlook into your Access table. You never have to touch the data with your hands, which means that you don't have to worry about making a mistake as you type the data. Yes, it's possible your colleague made a mistake while entering the data, but you reduce the number of steps in the process and eliminate many opportunities to introduce errors.

Send a Data Collection E-Mail Message

1. Click the table for which you want to collect data.
2. Click the External Data tab.
3. In the Collect Data group, click Create E-Mail.
4. Click Next to advance past the first Collect Data Through E-Mail Messages wizard page (not shown).
5. Select the HTML Form option.
6. Click Next.
7. Select the Collect New Information Only option.
8. Click Next.

(continued on the next page)

Caution

Both you and your recipient must have Microsoft Office Outlook 2007 installed to exchange data collection e-mail messages.

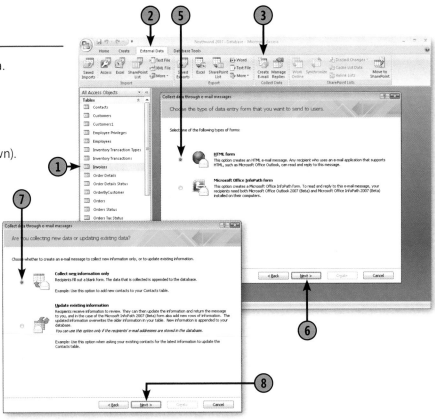

Send a Data Collection E-Mail Message *(continued)*

⑨ Click the first field you want to add to the form.

⑩ Click the Add button.

⑪ Repeat Steps 9 and 10 to add all applicable fields.

⑫ Click Next.

⑬ Verify that the Automatically Process Replies And Add Data To *Invoices* option is deselected.

⑭ Click Next.

⑮ Select the Enter The E-mail Addresses In Microsoft Office Outlook option.

⑯ Click Next.

⑰ Type a subject for the e-mail messages.

⑱ Type an introduction for the e-mail messages.

⑲ Click Next.

⑳ Click Create.

Caution

If you select the Automatically Process Replies And Add Data To *Table* option, Outlook exports any survey replies to your Access table when the messages arrive. However, if the database is open when Outlook attempts to write the data to your table, the operation will fail, and you will need to transfer the data manually.

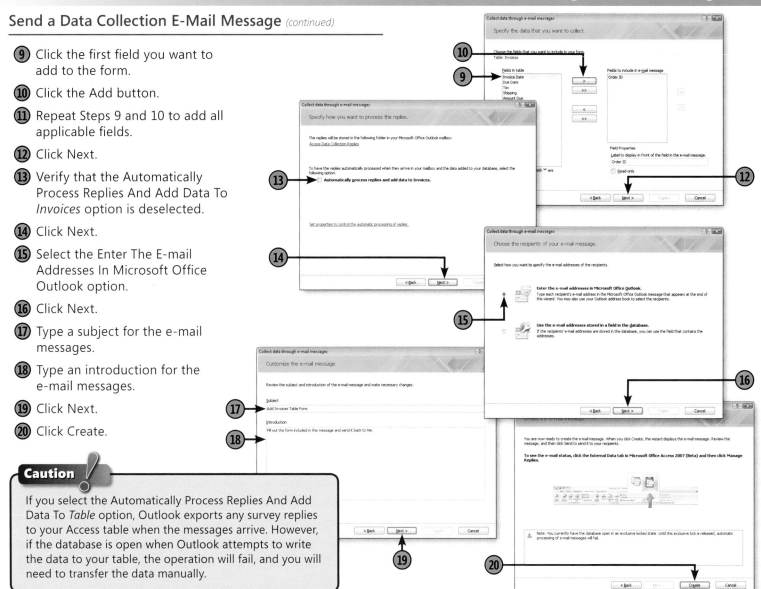

Process Data Collection
E-Mail Messages

① Close the Microsoft Office Access database into which you want to bring in the form data.

② In Microsoft Office Outlook, click the show detail control next to the Inbox mailbox name.

③ Click the Access Data Collection Replies folder.

④ Right-click the data collection message.

⑤ Click Export Data to Microsoft Office Access.

⑥ Click OK twice to export the data and to dismiss the message box that appears to indicate the data transfer was successful.

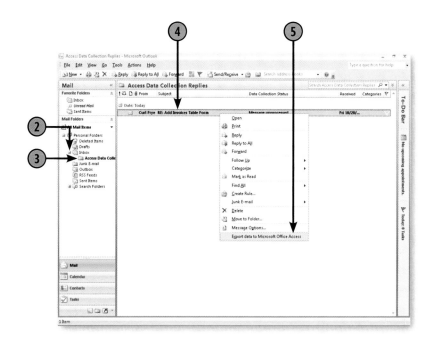

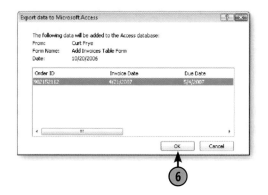

14

Administering a Database

When working with sensitive data, you need to ensure that only authorized individuals are able to read it. For example, if you manage a database containing your coworkers' salary information and performance reviews, you should do as much as you can to keep the database in good working order and ensure that no one has access to that information unless it is needed.

Microsoft Office Access 2007 has a range of security and administration tools you can use to protect sensitive data while still allowing folks with a legitimate need to get at the data with as little hassle as possible. Those tools range from requiring your colleagues to type passwords to use a database to the Documenter utility that prints the vital statistics of every object in your database.

Introducing Database Security

At their heart, databases are programs to store important data. Whether you're protecting your friends' privacy by ensuring no one else opens your contacts database or preventing your colleagues from accidentally modifying or deleting important business data, database security is a critical part of using Access on computers connected to a network.

Passwords

Because they're so important to good security, in Access and elsewhere, a quick note about passwords is in order. The best passwords are random strings of characters, but random characters are hard to remember. One good method of creating hard-to-guess passwords is to combine elements of two words, mixing uppercase and lowercase letters with a number in between to generate a character string that is at least eight characters long. For example, if you know something about horseback riding, you might have a password of StiRr03rt, which could be read

as "stirrups, three notches higher on the right." In any event, avoid passwords that are simple dictionary words in English or any other language, as they can easily be solved by password-guessing programs available on the Internet. Substituting numbers for letters in dictionary words, as in c00l, is no better as all substitutions are included in the password-guessing programs.

Encrypting Databases

Another technique you can use to prevent unauthorized users from getting at your data is to encrypt the database. When you create a database, the data and structural information used to create the database is stored as plain text, which can be read quickly and easily. The problem is that the same information can be read by opening the file in a word processor. So, even if you set user accounts and passwords for your database, it's still possible to read the underlying data. To prevent unauthorized viewing, you can scramble the information used to create the database. Access can read the data without difficulty, but the database runs about 10 to 15 percent slower because of the additional processing required.

Encrypting a Database

When you create an Access 2007 database, you should consider that it's possible to view and edit the contents of an Access database using a word processing program such as Microsoft Word. You don't see the tables in the same easy-to-use layout you get when you open the database in Access, but all the data is there. In other words, storing your database on a computer without Access 2007 is no guarantee your data is safe from prying eyes. Fortunately, obscuring the contents of your database, or encrypting the database, can be accomplished in just a few steps.

Encrypt a Database

1. Close any open databases.
2. Click the Microsoft Office button.
3. Click Open.
4. Click the database you want to open.
5. Click the down arrow at the right edge of the Open button.
6. Click Open Exclusive.
7. Click the Database Tools tab.
8. Click Encrypt with Password.
9. In the Set Database Password dialog box that appears, type your password.
10. Retype your password.
11. Click OK.

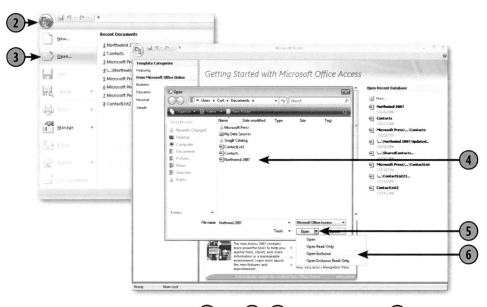

Caution

If you don't open your database in Exclusive mode, clicking the Encrypt with Password button causes Access 2007 to display a warning dialog box instructing you to close the database and reopen it in Exclusive mode.

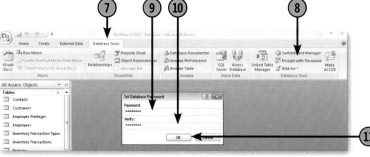

Decrypt a Database

① Click the Database Tools tab.

② Click Decrypt Database.

③ In the Unset Database Password dialog box, type the database's password.

④ Click OK.

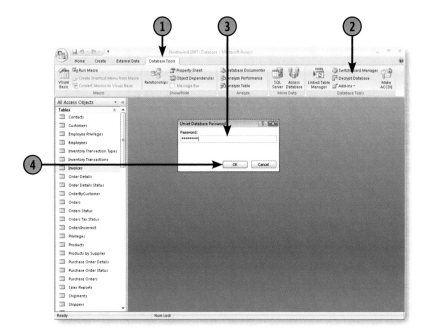

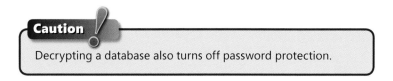

Caution

Decrypting a database also turns off password protection.

Locking Database Records

Forms are versatile objects—you can use them to browse a database table or your query results, or to enter or modify table records. There may be some forms, however, that let your colleagues peek into tables where the records are too important to be modified. To prevent accidents where important data gets deleted by well-meaning computer users, you can set a form's properties so the ability to add, modify, and delete records is turned off.

If more than one person is responsible for entering data into your database, you could run into a situation where more than one person attempts to enter or edit data using a form. Attempting to edit records simultaneously can result in data entry errors, so it's best to prevent a user from editing a record when another user is trying to do the same thing.

Prevent More than One User from Editing a Form Record

1. Open a form in Design view.
2. Double-click the form selector.
3. Click Data.
4. Click Record Locks.
5. Click the down arrow that appears.
6. Click Edited Record.

Tip

Clicking the Record Locks down arrow and then clicking All Records prevents users, including yourself, from making any changes to the form's data.

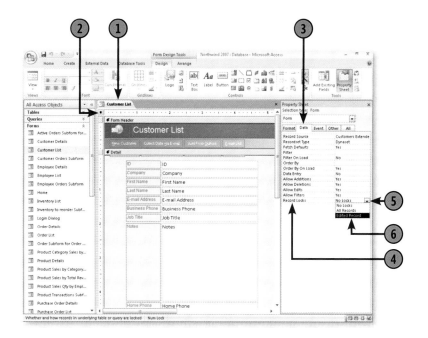

Lock Records in a Form

1. Open a form in Design view.

2. Double-click the form selector.

3. Click Data.

4. Follow these steps for the Allow Additions, Allow Deletions, and Allow Edits properties:

   ■ Click the property name.

   ■ Click the down arrow that appears.

   ■ Click No.

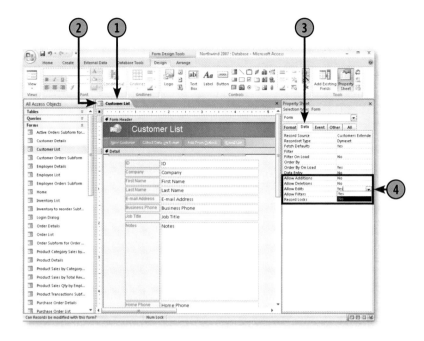

Creating a Switchboard

When you open some databases, a navigation form appears to help you find common tasks and data sources. This form, called a switchboard, contains controls you can click to view product and order information, print a sales report, open the database window, or even exit Access. If you create a database using a database wizard, the wizard creates a switchboard form for you. If you create a database from scratch, or if you delete the switchboard from a wizard-created database, you can build your own switchboard. In either case, you can edit the switchboard to add, delete, or modify the controls available on the first or subsequent pages.

Create a Switchboard

① Click the Database Tools tab.

② Click Switchboard Manager.

③ Click Yes to have Access 2007 create a new switchboard form.

④ Click Close.

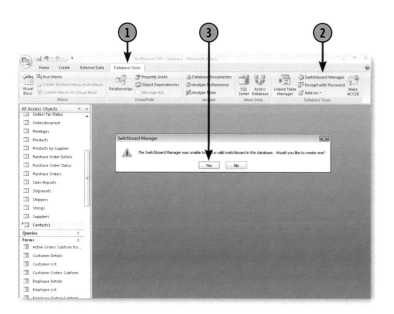

Add a Switchboard Page

① Click the Database Tools tab.

② Click Switchboard Manager.

③ Click New.

④ Type a name for the page.

⑤ Click OK.

⑥ Click Close.

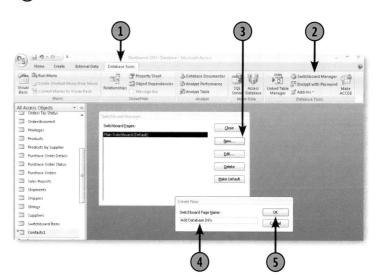

Add an Item to a Switchboard Page

① Click the Database Tools tab.

② Click Switchboard Manager.

③ Click the page to which you want to add an item.

④ Click Edit.

⑤ Click New.

⑥ Type the text to appear next in the item.

⑦ Click the Command down arrow.

⑧ Click the command you want to assign to the item.

⑨ Click the bottom box's down arrow.

⑩ Click the item that is the target of the command.

⑪ Click OK.

⑫ Click Close to close the Edit Switchboard Page dialog box.

⑬ Click Close to close the Switchboard Manager.

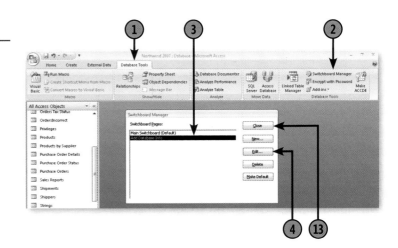

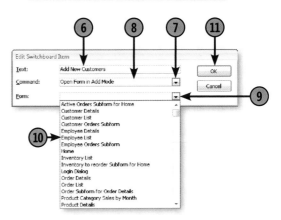

Tip

You can delete a switchboard page or an item by clicking it and then clicking the Delete button.

Tip

Switchboard commands can refer to actions such as exiting Access 2007, closing the current database, or opening a form or report. The name of the final list of available objects or actions will change to reflect the command you choose.

Documenting a Database

Keeping track of every table, query, and report in a database isn't that hard when the database is new and fresh in your memory, but as you add new objects and move on to other projects, it can be hard to remember everything about your database. Access can document the properties of selected objects in your database by running the Documenter. In the Documenter, you can choose the objects you want to get information about and then print a report, which gives you both a hard copy of your database in case something goes wrong and a report you can pass on to a programmer or administrator should you move on to other projects.

Document a Database

1. Click the Database Tools tab.

2. Click Database Documenter.

3. Click the dialog box tab representing the objects you want to document.

4. Follow any of these steps to select the objects you want to document:

   ■ Select the check box next to an object to select the object (you can also click an object's name and then click the Select button).

   ■ Click Select All to select every listed object.

   ■ Click Deselect All to remove all of your previous selections.

5. Click OK.

Try This!

Open the Northwind 2007 sample database and click the Database Tools tab. In the Analyze group, click Database Documenter to display the Documenter dialog box. In the Documenter dialog box, click the Tables tab, click the Employees table, click Select, and then click OK. Access 2007 creates a report detailing the selected objects.

Caution

If you document every element of your database, the printed report could be extremely long.

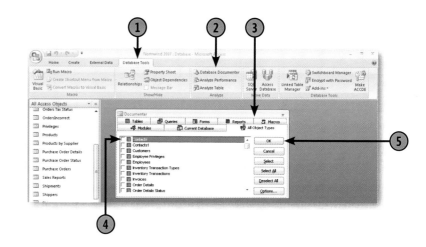

Setting Startup Options

When you create a database for you and your colleagues to enter data, you may want to limit what your colleagues can do with the database. Locking records and assigning database passwords provide some restrictions, but you can also set which form appears when you start the database. When you create a database where users see only a designated form at startup, you've created an application.

Change an Application Title

① Click the Microsoft Office button.

② Click Access Options.

③ Click Current Database.

④ Type a title for the Application.

⑤ Click OK.

> **Caution**
>
> Clicking (None) on the Display Form/Page drop-down list means no form opens when you or your colleagues run the database. If you hide the database window on startup, your colleagues won't be able to view the database's contents!

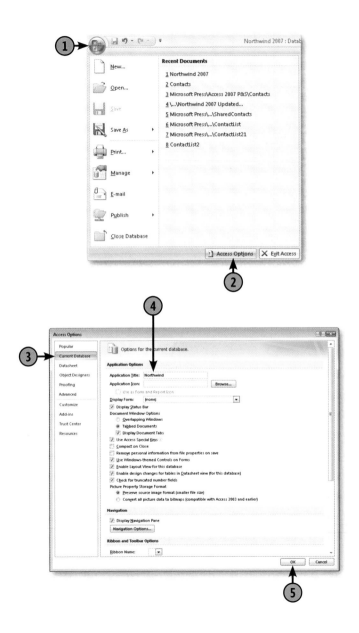

Hide All Menus

1 Click the Microsoft Office button.

2 Click Access Options.

3 Click Current Database.

4 In the Ribbon and Toolbar Options section, deselect the Allow Full Menus check box.

5 Deselect the Allow Default Shortcut Menus check box.

6 Click OK.

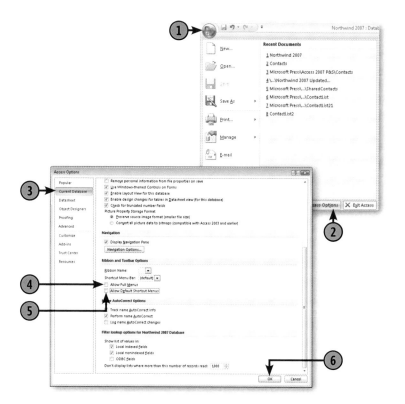

Set Startup Form

1 Click the Microsoft Office button.

2 Click Access Options.

3 Click Current Database.

4 In the Application Options section, click the Display Form down arrow.

5 Click the form you want to appear when the database opens.

6 Click OK.

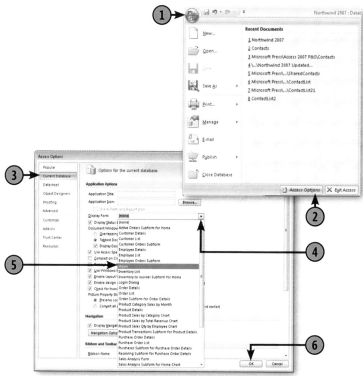

Set Startup Display Options

① Click the Microsoft Office button.

② Click Access Options.

③ Click Current Database.

④ Deselect the Display Status Bar check box to hide the status bar.

⑤ Deselect the Display Document Tabs check box to hide the tabs of open documents.

⑥ Deselect the Enable Layout View for this Database check box to prevent users from displaying forms and reports in Layout view.

⑦ In the Navigation section, deselect the Display Navigation Pane check box to prevent users from displaying the database's objects.

⑧ Click OK.

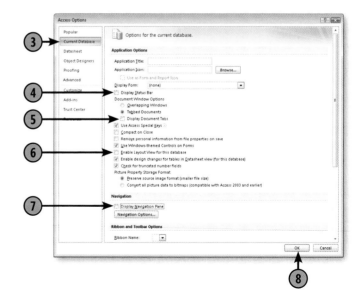

15

Customizing Access

Microsoft Office Access 2007 is designed so you can create and use your databases quickly and easily. As you get more familiar with the program, you may find that you perform some tasks more frequently than others, or that you'd work more effectively if the Quick Access Toolbar was set up a little differently. You can modify how Access presents itself to you to make your work flow quickly.

One way you can change the Access interface is to add or remove buttons from the Quick Access Toolbar. Clicking the Customize Quick Access Toolbar button, located at the right edge of the Quick Access Toolbar, shows a list of all buttons available for that toolbar. If there are buttons on the Quick Access Toolbar that you don't use as much as you used to, it's no trouble to remove them. Also, if you find yourself using the same group of controls on a ribbon tab, you can add those groups to the Quick Access Toolbar and reduce the number of clicks it takes to activate those controls. Finally, you can automate repetitive tasks by creating macros or a series of actions you can create and run whenever you need to.

Adding Buttons to the Quick Access Toolbar

When you install Microsoft Access, the user interface is set up so that the controls you click to perform your tasks are easy to find and, just as importantly, grouped together on the ribbon. After you work with the program for a while, though, you may find that you use some controls much more often than others. In that case, you can add individual controls, or entire groups of controls, to the Quick Access Toolbar at the top of the ribbon. If your needs change and you find you don't need those controls on the Quick Access Toolbar, you can remove them just as easily as you added them.

Add a Button

① Click the Customize Quick Access Toolbar button.

② Click More Commands.

③ Click the Choose Commands From down arrow.

④ Click the desired category.

⑤ Click the command you want to add.

⑥ Click Add.

⑦ Click OK.

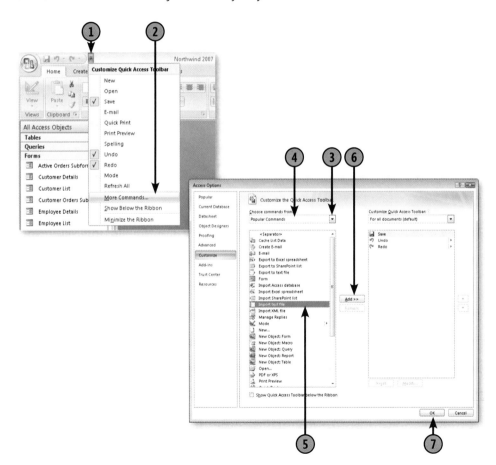

Remove a Button

① Right-click the button you want to remove.

② Click Remove from Quick Access Toolbar.

Add a Group

① Right-click the group label of the group you want to add to the ribbon.

② Click Add to Quick Access Toolbar.

Remove a Group

① Right-click the group you want to remove.

② Click Remove from Quick Access Toolbar.

Tip

You can change the Quick Access Toolbar back to its original configuration by clicking the Customize Quick Access Toolbar button and then clicking More Commands. Then, on the Customize page of the Access Options dialog box, click Reset and then click OK.

Building a Macro

A macro is a series of automated steps, such as opening a report or form or displaying a message box that you create and save. After you save the macro, you can run it whenever you want, either by right-clicking it and clicking the Run option, or by running it when something specific happens, such as clicking a button on a form. If you export Access tables to other formats, print records, or search for records and are tired of going through the process manually, you can create a macro that does it for you.

Create a Macro

① Click the Create tab.

② Click the top part of the Macro button.

③ Click the down arrow in the first Action cell.

④ Click the desired action.

⑤ Fill in the arguments for the action. The arguments you can set will be different for every action.

- Repeat Steps 3 through 5 on subsequent table rows to add actions to your macro.

⑥ On the Quick Access Toolbar, click the Save button.

⑦ In the Save As dialog box that appears, type a name for your macro.

⑧ Click OK.

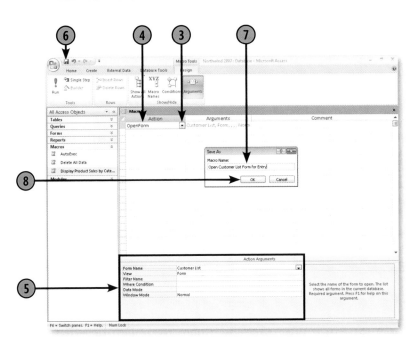

Running a Macro

Once you create a macro, you can run it (that is, have Access execute the macro's steps) several ways. The most straightforward way to run a macro is to display the macros in your database, click the one you want to run, and then click the Run button. If a macro doesn't do what you expect, or if you're just curious to see how it works, you can step through the macro one action at a time. While you step through the macro, Access lets you know what's going on so you can learn what the macro's doing and either fix a problem or apply what you learn to macros you create on your own.

Run a Macro

1. If necessary, in the Navigation Pane, click the Macros header.

2. Right-click the macro you want to run.

3. Click Run.

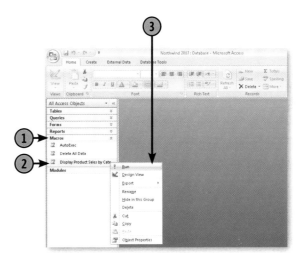

See Also

For more information about launching a macro when a form is opened, see "Running a Macro When a Form Opens" on page 243.

Step through a Macro

1 If necessary, in the Navigation Pane, click the Macros header.

2 Right-click the macro you want to step through.

3 Click Design View.

4 Click the Single Step button.

5 Click the Run button to execute the first macro action.

6 Follow any of these steps:

■ Click Step to execute the next macro step.

■ Click Stop All Macros to stop running the macro (and any other macros that might be running).

■ Click Continue to run the macro without pausing between steps.

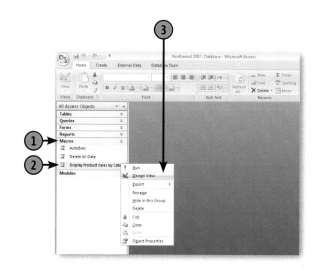

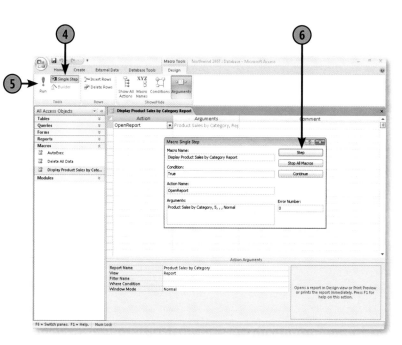

Tip ✓

If you work with a macro in a new database, taking the time to step through the macro can teach you a lot about the database and its structure.

Caution !

If you click the Single Step button, the macro runs in Single Step mode until you click the Single Step button again.

Defining Macro Groups

After you get the hang of creating macros and discover how much time they can save you, you'll probably create lots of macros to print table contents, import data, or run searches. Managing dozens of macro files can take lots of time and energy, but there is an easier way! If you create a series of macros that are related by the objects they work on or the actions they perform, you can save the macros in a single file and identify individual macros by their name. In a way, defining a macro group is like having a bunch of files in a directory—when the macros are grouped by theme, or by the name of the form from which they run, they're that much easier to find.

Create a Macro Group

1. If necessary, in the Navigation Pane, click the Macros header.

2. Right-click the macro file you want to define as a group.

3. Click Design View.

4. Click the Macro Names button.

5. Type the name for the first macro.

6. Click the second cell in the Action column.

7. Click the down arrow.

8. Click the Action to be taken in this macro step.

9. Repeat Steps 6 through 8 in subsequent rows of the design grid to add macro actions.

10. In the Macro Name cell below the last action in the previous macro, type the name of the next macro to be stored in the group.

11. Repeat Steps 6 through 8 in subsequent rows of the design grid to add actions to the second macro.

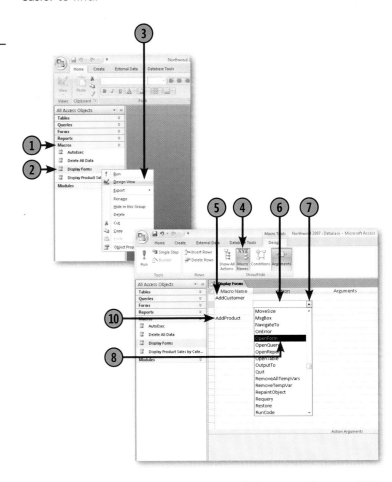

Adding and Deleting Macro Actions

Macros are a great way to do whatever you want with Access, but there may be times when you want to extend a macro's capabilities. Perhaps you forgot to open a form in your macro, want to open a new form you just created, or just want to add a blank line to the design grid so your macro is easier to read. To add a blank line to a macro, all you need to do is click the Insert Rows button. By the same token, you can remove an existing action or blank line from a macro by clicking the Delete Rows button. None of your changes is finalized until you save the macro, so if anything goes wrong, you can close the macro without saving your changes.

Insert a Macro Step

① If necessary, in the Navigation Pane, click the Macros header.

② Right-click the macro to which you want to add a step.

③ Click Design View.

④ Click any cell in the row below where you want the new row to appear.

⑤ Click the Insert Rows button.

⑥ Click the Save button.

Tip

It's a good idea to leave a row or two between the actions in your macros. That way, if you want to insert an action between two existing actions, you can do it without having to rearrange everything.

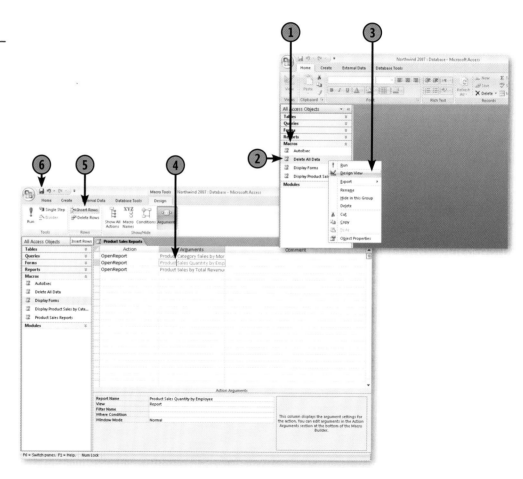

Delete a Macro Step

(1) If necessary, in the Navigation Pane, click the Macros header.

(2) Right-click the macro in which you want to delete a step.

(3) Click Design View.

(4) Click any cell in the row with the step you want to delete.

(5) Click the Delete Rows button.

(6) Click the Save button.

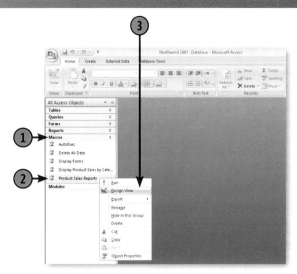

Tip ✓

If you have trouble with a macro and want Access to skip a step, you don't have to delete the step and re-create it later. Instead, just click the Conditions button to display the Condition column and type False in the Condition cell of the step you want to skip. When you're ready to run the step again, delete the word False and you're set!

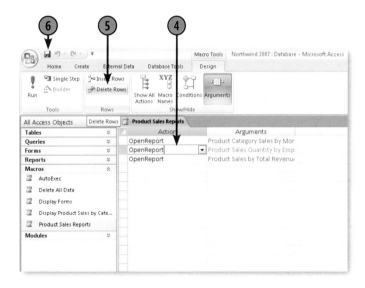

Launching a Macro from a Button

You and your colleagues can run any macro any time you want by right-clicking it and clicking the Run option, but there is a better way to let your colleagues run a macro whenever they want. To do that, you can create a command button on a form and tell Access to run the macro whenever someone clicks the button. The Main Switchboard form that appears when you open the Northwind sample database has several such buttons that let you print sales reports or open the main database window.

Assign a Macro to a Button

① Open a form in Design view.

② If necessary, click the Design tab.

③ If necessary, click the Control Wizards button.

④ Click the Button control.

⑤ Click the location in the Detail section where you want the command button to appear.

⑥ Click Miscellaneous.

⑦ Click Run Macro.

⑧ Click Next.

(continued on the next page)

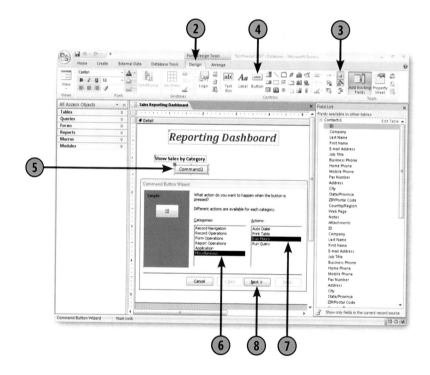

Assign a Macro to a Button *(continued)*

⑨ Click the macro you want to run when a user clicks the command button.

⑩ Click Next.

⑪ Select the Text option.

⑫ Type the text to appear on the command button's face.

⑬ Type a name for the button, and click Finish.

Tip

If you want to disable a command button without removing it from a form, you can do so by setting the button's Enabled property to "No." To do that, open the form in Design view, right-click the command button, and choose Properties from the shortcut menu. In the Property Sheet task pane that appears, click the Data tab, click the Enabled down arrow, and click No in the list. Click the Close box to close the Property Sheet task pane. To enable the command button, set the Enabled Property to "Yes."

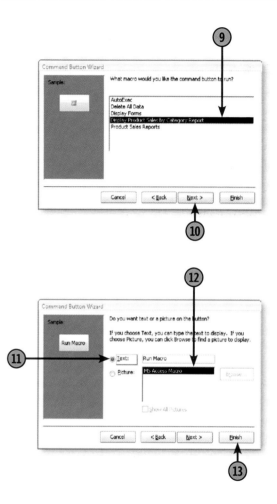

Displaying a Message Box

One useful thing you can do with macros is to display a message box indicating what folks should expect to see while using your database. Your message box can have a message of up to 255 characters, giving you plenty of room to explain what sort of data to enter into a field, to give your colleague advice on the purpose of a form, or to indicate the last time a form was modified.

Create a Message Box

① Click the Create tab.

② Click the top part of the Macro button.

③ Click the first cell in the Action column.

④ Click the down arrow.

⑤ Click MsgBox.

⑥ Type the text to appear in the Message box.

⑦ Click Type.

⑧ Click the down arrow.

⑨ Click the type of message box you want to appear.

⑩ Type the text to appear on the title bar of the message box.

⑪ Click the Save button.

⑫ In the Save As dialog box that appears, type a name for the macro.

⑬ Click OK.

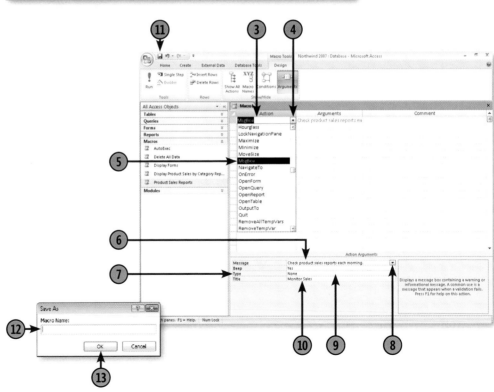

Running a Macro When a Form Opens

The best form designs put as much data as possible on the page, but it's also important that the data be readable. After all, if you cram every field together on a form, you might as well display the data as a datasheet! One way to give you and your colleagues information about how a form works without taking up any of your form's "real estate" is to display a message box when the form opens. By having the message box appear at the start, you ensure that your message is seen without getting in the way of the data on the form.

Run a Macro When a Form Opens

1 Open a form in Design view.

2 Double-click the form selector.

3 Click the Event tab.

4 Click On Open.

5 Click the down arrow.

6 Click the macro you want to run when the form opens.

See Also

For more information about creating a macro that displays a message box, see "Displaying a Message Box" on page 242.

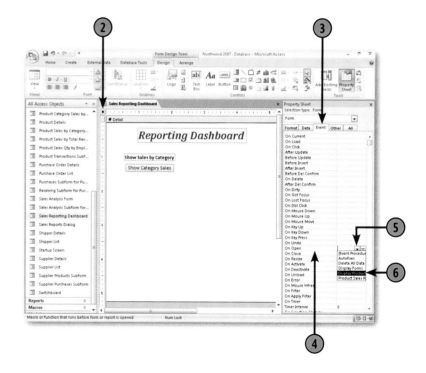

Changing AutoCorrect Options

You're bound to make typing mistakes when you spend a lot of time at the keyboard. In fact, slowing down doesn't help; the slower you go, the more likely you are to hit the wrong keys as you try to guide your fingers to the keys using your eyes instead of letting your muscle memory take over. Over the years, many users have allowed the programming team to monitor their typing, which means that the Access team has been able to identify the most common mistakes resulting from popular misspellings, letter transpositions, and errors that are the result of not hitting the spacebar fast enough to put a space between words. If one of the words Access identifies as an error is actually correct (for example, you work with a client corporation named Idae, a popular misspelling of the word idea), you can delete that entry from the AutoCorrect list.

Tip ✓

Many users type the same text frequently, such as "Payment is due within 30 days. If payment is made within 10 days, you may deduct 2% from the total amount due." If you often type that text, you could create an AutoCorrect entry that replaces the phrase Net30_2 with the text describing the payment terms listed.

Change AutoCorrect Options

1. Click the Microsoft Office button.

2. Click Access Options.

3. Click Proofing.

4. Click AutoCorrect Options.

5. Deselect the check boxes next to the rules you want to turn off or select the check boxes next to the rules you want to turn on.

6. Click OK to close the AutoCorrect dialog box.

7. Click OK to close the Access Options dialog box.

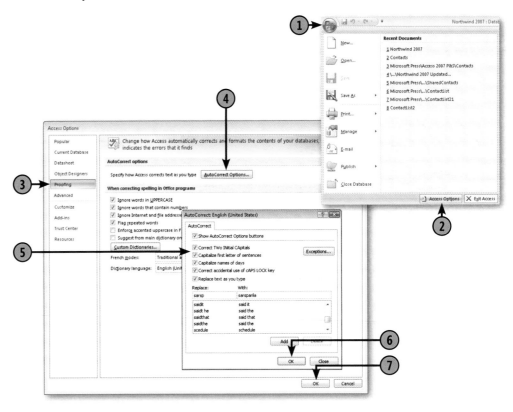

Tip ✓

To undo an AutoCorrect correction, press Ctrl+Z.

Add AutoCorrect Rules

① Click the Microsoft Office button.

② Click Access Options.

③ Click Proofing.

④ Click AutoCorrect Options.

⑤ Type the text to be replaced.

⑥ Type the text to replace the previous entry.

⑦ Click Add.

⑧ Click OK to close the AutoCorrect dialog box.

⑨ Click OK to close the Access Options dialog box.

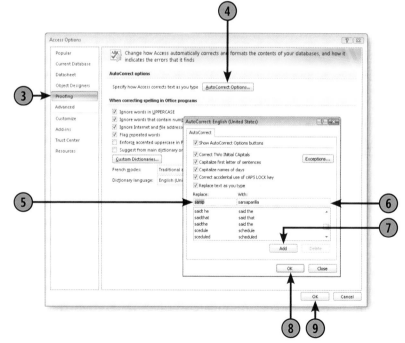

Delete an AutoCorrect Entry

① Click the Microsoft Office button.

② Click Access Options.

③ Click Proofing.

④ Click AutoCorrect Options.

⑤ Click the entry to be removed.

⑥ Click Delete.

⑦ Click OK to close the AutoCorrect dialog box.

⑧ Click OK to close the Access Options dialog box.

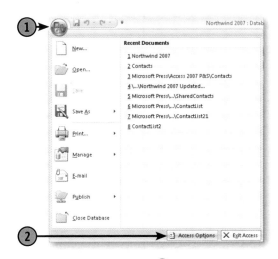

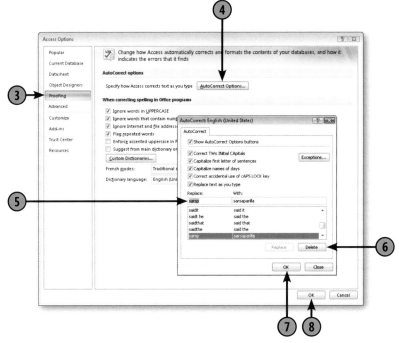

Presenting Table and Query Data Dynamically

The capabilities Microsoft Office Access 2007 places at your disposal are wide-ranging and powerful. You can build tables to store data effectively, ask questions of the data using queries, and display the data in forms and reports. What's even better, you can use many of those techniques in a single database object: the PivotTable Report.

When you create a PivotTable, you build a versatile object you can use as part of live business presentations to illustrate your own points and answer your colleagues' questions quickly. If you'd rather summarize your data visually, you can create Pivot-Chart Reports, which let you reorganize and redisplay your data in a chart.

Introducing PivotTables and PivotCharts

Microsoft Access 2007 gives you a lot of flexibility in choosing how to present your data. The most basic method of presenting your data is in a table, where the data is listed one row at a time. Displaying your data in a form lets you present the data one record at a time; reports give you the additional ability to organize your table contents or query results based on grouping levels. Finally, if one field in your table or query is related to two other fields in the table or query, such as with sales data for the quantity of a given product sold in a month, you can create a crosstab query to present the data in relation to the other fields.

PivotTables let you combine all of these abilities into a single database object, with some added benefits thrown in.

Not only can you present your data in an easily understood format, you can change the data's organization while you have the PivotTable open. As with other database objects, Access steps you through the PivotTable creation process with a wizard that explains everything you need to do.

Pivoting

When you open a form that contains a PivotTable, your data appears in a layout that is very similar to that of a crosstab query. PivotTables add to this by enabling you to reorganize the data in the PivotTable by moving the field heads to reflect the desired layout.

Field heads

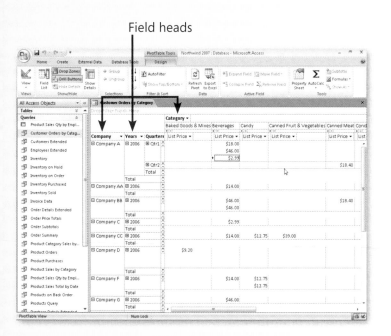

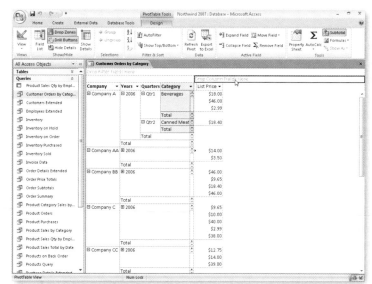

Filtering

When you work with large data collections, it's important that you be able to limit the data that appears on the screen. With PivotTables, you can click the down arrow at the right edge of a field head and choose the values to display.

Once you choose the values you want to concentrate on, clicking OK limits the contents of the PivotTable to the items you selected.

PivotCharts

Just as you can create PivotTables, which let you reorganize your table data, you can create PivotCharts to summarize your data graphically. As with a PivotTable, you can change how the PivotChart presents your data, both by reorganizing the data and by changing the PivotChart's chart type.

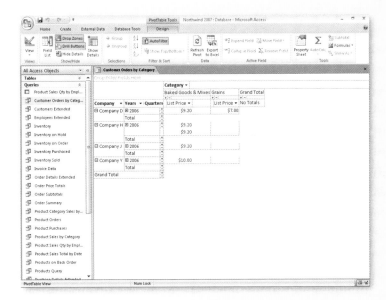

Creating a PivotTable

Access databases let you gather and present important data, but the standard table only shows a list of values. Forms and reports let you summarize and display your data so it's easier to evaluate, but you're still limited to a single view of your data. Even queries, which let you perform calculations on your data or present it in a crosstab worksheet, give you a single view of your data. PivotTables, by contrast, let you rearrange your data dynamically. If your PivotTable lists sales by category and you'd rather see the data organized by country, you can change the layout of your PivotTable quickly. Once you create your first PivotTable, you understand how powerful a tool they are!

Create a PivotTable Form

① Click the table or query that contains the data you want to summarize in your PivotTable.

② Click the Create tab.

③ Click More Forms.

④ Click PivotTable. If necessary, click the Field List button.

(continued on the next page)

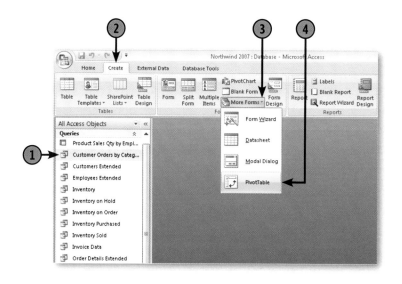

Tip

You should add every field from the table or query you're using to your PivotTable. You won't need to use all of the fields in the PivotTable, but they are available if you do want them.

See Also

For information about using the Drop Filter Fields Here area, see "Filtering PivotTable Data" on page 255.

Create a PivotTable Form *(continued)*

⑤ Drag fields that you want to provide values for the PivotTable's rows from the PivotTable Field List box to the Drop Row Fields Here area.

⑥ Drag fields that you want to provide values for the PivotTable's columns from the PivotTable Field List box to the Drop Column Fields Here area.

⑦ Drag the fields that you want to provide values for the body of the Pivot-Table from the PivotTable Field List box to the Drop Totals or Detail Fields Here area.

⑧ Click the Save button.

⑨ Type a name for the PivotTable form.

⑩ Click OK.

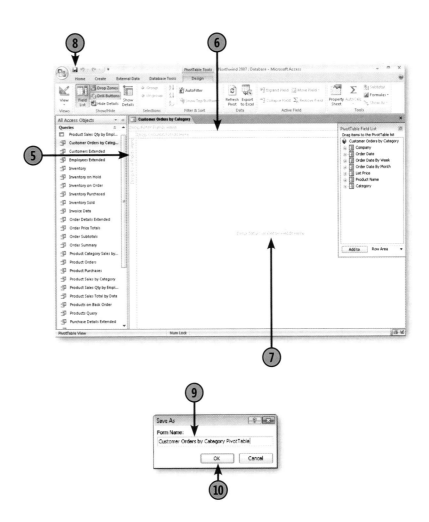

Tip

When you create a PivotTable, you should make sure "PivotTable" appears in the name of the form you create to hold it. It doesn't change how the form operates, but it does make it easier to find.

Adding and Removing PivotTable Fields

After you create a PivotTable, you can arrange the fields on the PivotTable to present your data effectively. It is possible your colleagues could ask questions you hadn't thought of, but that you could answer if you included another field in the Pivot-Table and used it to filter or organize your data. Maybe they're interested in how dairy products have been selling in South America. While you didn't include the countries for each

sale in the original PivotTable design, that data is in the query on which you based the PivotTable. All you need to do is add it to the design. By the same token, you can remove any fields you're not using. You can drag them from the body of the PivotTable to the PivotTable Field List box, ready for use if you need them again.

Add a Field to a PivotTable

1. Display the forms in your database.

2. Double-click the PivotTable form.

3. If necessary, click the Field List button.

4. Drag the field you want to the desired spot on the PivotTable.

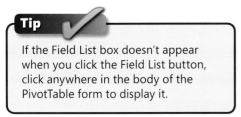

Tip

If the Field List box doesn't appear when you click the Field List button, click anywhere in the body of the PivotTable form to display it.

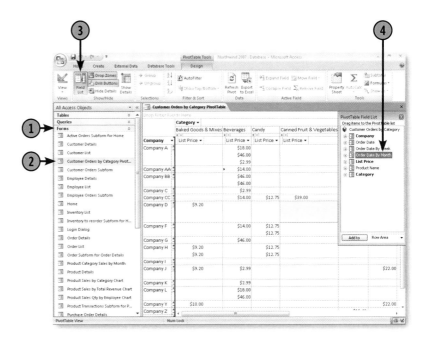

Remove a Field from a PivotTable

① Display the forms in your database.

② Double-click the PivotTable form.

③ Right-click the field header of the field you want to remove.

④ Click Remove.

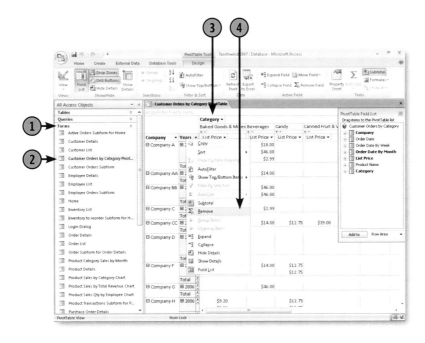

Pivoting a PivotTable

Perhaps the biggest benefit of presenting your data using PivotTables is that you can change the data's organization on the fly, creating literally dozens of different forms from a single data set! All you have to do is drag the header of the field you want to move to its new position—when you release the mouse button Access examines the PivotTable's new structure and rearranges the data to match it. If previously you had listed sales by Country and then by product Category, you could drag the Category field header to the left of the Country field header to reverse the grouping.

Reorganize PivotTable Data

① Display the forms in your database.

② Double-click the PivotTable form.

③ Drag the header you want to relocate to the desired position in the PivotTable.

Tip ✓

If you use a lot of fields in your Pivot-Table, you might not be able to remember the exact ordering of fields that produce a particular arrangement. When you find an arrangement that presents your data effectively, send yourself an e-mail message with the order or record the arrangement in a Word document so you can re-create the arrangement quickly.

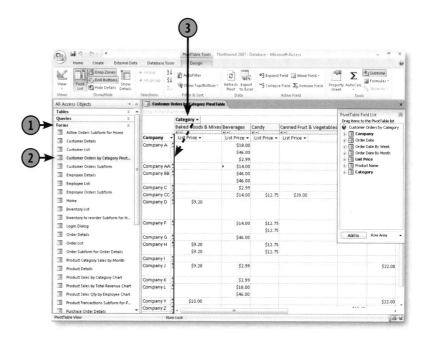

Filtering PivotTable Data

When you create a PivotTable from the data in your tables or queries, you often have several screens worth of data to move through. Reorganizing your data can help you interpret your data, but you can also filter your PivotTable by choosing the data you want to see. For example, if your PivotTable shows sales data for a series of products grouped by category, you can pick the categories for which you want to view data.

Select Which Field Values to Display

1. Display the forms in your database.

2. Double-click the PivotTable form.

3. Click the down arrow on the header of the field by which you want to filter.

4. Deselect the All check box to clear the check boxes for all values.

5. Select the check box next to any value you want to display.

6. Click OK.

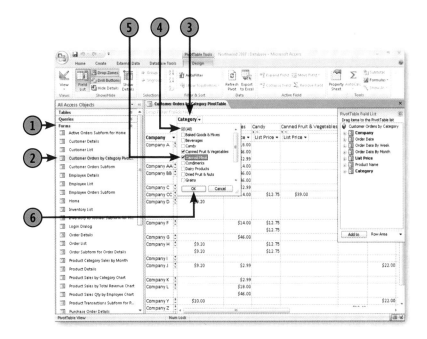

Tip

If you're not sure whether all values in a field are displayed, look at the field's header. The down arrow will be blue if the field has a filter applied to it.

Filter by a Field Not Displayed in the Body of a PivotTable

① Display the forms in your database.

② Double-click the PivotTable form.

③ If necessary, click the Field List button.

④ Drag the field by which you want to filter the PivotTable to the Drop Filter Fields Here area.

⑤ Click the down arrow on the field header.

⑥ Deselect the All check box.

⑦ Select the check box next to each value to display.

⑧ Click OK.

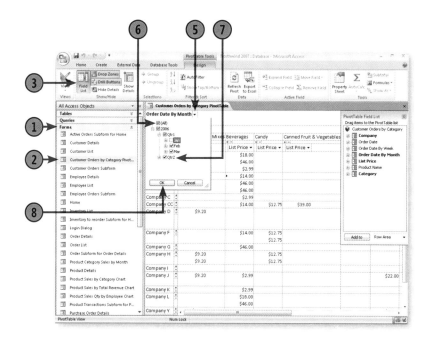

Toggle a Filter On and Off

① Click the AutoFilter button to remove a filter.

② Click the AutoFilter button again to reapply the filter.

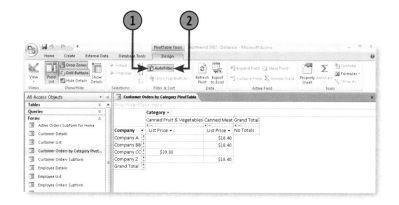

Formatting a PivotTable

PivotTables are all about presenting your data effectively, and a significant element of any presentation is the appearance of your data. To change the appearance of an element of your PivotTable, such as the color, pattern, and font, you use the Properties box.

Change a PivotTable's Appearance

1 Display the forms in your database.

2 Double-click the PivotTable form.

3 Click the part of the PivotTable you want to format.

4 Click the Property Sheet button.

5 Set the format you want in the Properties box.

6 Click the Close box.

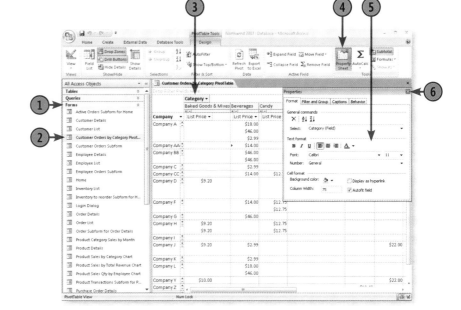

Creating a PivotChart

Just as you can create tables that you can reorganize on the fly to emphasize different aspects of your table and query data, you can also create dynamic charts, or PivotCharts, to summarize your data effectively. By changing the grouping order of the fields used to create your PivotChart, or by limiting which values are presented in the PivotChart, you answer specific questions posed by you and your colleagues. In addition to letting you change how your data appears in the chart, you can even change the type of chart you use to display your data!

Step through the PivotChart Wizard

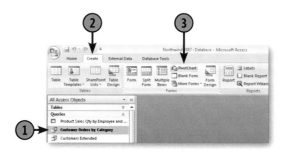

① Click the database object that contains your PivotChart data.

② Click the Create tab.

③ Click PivotChart.

④ Drag fields that you want to provide values for the PivotChart's category axis rows from the Chart Field List box to the Drop Category Fields Here area.

⑤ Drag fields that you want to provide values for the PivotChart's data series from the Chart Field List box to the Drop Series Fields Here area.

⑥ Drag the fields that you want to provide values for the body of the PivotChart from the Chart Field List box to the Drop Data Fields Here area.

⑦ Click the Save button.

(continued on the next page)

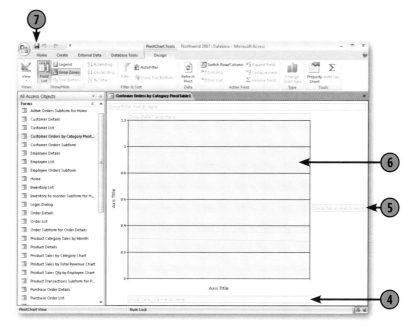

Step through the PivotChart Wizard *(continued)*

⑧ Type a name for your PivotChart.

⑨ Click OK.

Change a PivotChart Chart Type

① Display the forms in your database.

② Double-click the form that contains your PivotChart.

③ If necessary, click the Design tab.

④ Click the Change Chart Type button.

⑤ Click the Type tab.

⑥ Click the new chart type.

⑦ Click the subtype of the chart you want to create.

⑧ Click the Close box.

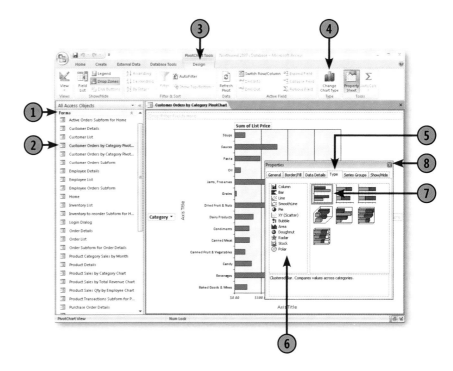

Index

Print Preview view, 30
Proofing command, 75–76
properties, fields, 53, 153
Property Sheet task pane, 91, 153, 241
publishing data, 214–15

Q

queries, 16, 101–23
    action queries, 103
    arithmetic operators, 112
    calculating values, 113
    comparison operators, 112
    creating, 110
    criteria, 111
    crosstab queries, 103, 120–21
    defined, 101
    detail queries, 104–05
    duplicates, finding, 114–15
    editing, 108–10
    fields, adding, 104, 109
    largest values, finding, 122
    logical operators, 112
    make-table queries, 103, 118
    opening, 108
    operators, 112
    parameter queries, 102
    select queries, 26, 102
    smallest values, finding, 123
    summary queries, 106–07
    tables, adding, 108
    tables, multiple, 109
    text strings, 111
    types, 102–03
    unmatched records, 116–17
    Update, 119
    updating table values, 119
    values, calculating, 113
    values, finding, 122–23

queries, continued
    viewing, 26
    Wizard, 104–07
    writing to table, 118
Queries command, 26
query object views, 30
Query Wizard, 104–07
    detail queries, 104–05
    summary queries, 106–07
Quick Access Toolbar, 77, 232–33
    buttons, adding, 232–33
    buttons, removing, 233
    groups, adding, 233
    groups, removing, 233

R

raw data, 170
record navigation bar, 23
Record Number box, record navigation
    bar, 23
records, 22
    creating, 24
    filtering, 84–86
    grouping, 27, 135–37
    locking, 223–24
    moving, 51
    sorting, 27
Records group, Home tab, 6, 22
Rectangle control, 96
referential integrity, 48
Relationships command, 46, 48
relationships, tables, 44–48
    bridging, 45
    defining, 46–47
    deleting, 46
    foreign key fields, 47
    many-to-many, 44–45
    one-to-many, 44

relationships, tables, continued
    primary keys, 46–47
    queries, 109
    referential integrity, 48
    transition tables, 45
Relationships window, 46, 48
Rename Column command, 81
Rename option, shortcut menu, 11
replacing text, 73
Report Footer, 135
Report Header, 135
report object views, 30
reports, 16, 27
    building, 130
    calculated fields, 134
    controls, 132–33
    creating, 125–41
    Design view, 130
    editing, 131
    Field List Task pane, 131
    fields, adding, 131
    gridlines, 157
    grouping level, 136–37
    Label Wizard, 141
    mailing labels, 140–41
    modifying, 131
    multiple fields, selecting, 129
    records, grouping, 135–37
    Report Wizard, 126–27
    rows, coloring, 158
    sections, 135
    subreports, 138–39
    summary, 128–29
    values, 134
Reports command, 27
Report view, 30
Report Wizard, 126–27
required fields/data entry, 59–60
Restore button, 12
ribbon, 5–6, 12

Rich Text group, Home tab, 6
rows, 22, 51, 82. *See also* records
    coloring, 158
    height, changing, 82
    macros, between, 238
    Totals, 159

S

Save As menu, 35
Save button, 22, 24
scrolling within database objects, 14
Search button, Help, 18
sections, reports, 135
security, 220–24
select queries, 26, 102
Selected Fields pane, Report
    Wizard, 127
sensitive information, 15, 56
shadow special effect, controls, 150
Shift+Tab keys, 23
shortcut, creating, 11
shortcut menus, Help, 17
Show Detail control, 16, 40
Shutter Bar, 16–17, 21–22, 24–27, 41
Single Step mode, 236
size, charts, 173
Snap to Grid button, 153
Sort & Filter group, Home tab, 6
sources, images, 163
spelling, 64
split forms, 100
SQL view, 30
Standard toolbar, 172, 175
Start button, 11
Start menu, 11
starting program, 11
startup form, 229
startup options, 228–30

status bar, 12
storing data, 10
style, charts, 173
subdatasheets, 10, 83
subforms, 98–99
Subform/Subreport control, 96, 98
Subform Wizard, 98
subreports, 138–39
summary queries, 106–07
summary reports, 128–29
switchboards, 25, 225–26
    adding items, 226
    adding pages, 225
    creating, 225
Switchboard command, 25
Switchboard Manager, 225
system resources, 15

T

Tab delimiter, 205
Tab key, 23
Tab page control, 96
table object views, 30
tables, 16
    adding to queries, 108
    backup copies, 50
    controls, 23
    copying, 42–43
    creating, 36–38
    customizing, 71–86
    Datasheet view, 50
    deselecting, 43
    design, 32–33
    Design view, 36–38, 50
    field descriptions, 36
    fields, adding, 39–40, 50–51
    fields, arranging, 51
    fields, deleting, 50

tables, *continued*
    foreign keys, 33
    ID fields, 33
    importing, 190–91
    linking to other database, 192–93
    multiple, queries, 109
    navigating, 23
    number per objects, 32
    primary keys, 33, 36–37
    records, filtering, 84–86
    relationships, 44–48
    removing, design grid, 110
    text, finding, 72
    text, replacing, 73
    typing data, 38
    viewing, 22
Tables command, Shutter Bar, 22, 41
Tables and Related Views command, 17
Table Templates button, Create tab, 39
tabs, ribbon, 6, 12
tabs, window, 16
Tabular form, 89
templates, 28–29
    database creation from, 28
    online, 29
"Text", 55
Text box control, 96
text data type, 52
text
    adding with AutoCorrect, 74
    exporting from file, 199–201
    formatting, 144
text boxes, charts, 177
text, tables
    adding, 77–79
    copying and pasting, 78–79
    deleting, 77
    finding, 72
    replacing, 73
    selecting, 77

text, tables, *continued*
   strings, queries, 111
   undoing operations, 77
textures, 166
tiling, pictures, 166
title bar, 12
Toggle button control, 96
Totals rows, 159
transition tables, 45
Try This! exercises
   AutoCorrect, 76
   controls distribution, 152
   documenting databases, 227
   filtering, 86
   Find Unmatched Query Wizard, 117
   forms, creating, 91
   indexing field values, 62
   report creation, 130
typing data, tables, 38

U

Unbound object frame control, 96
underline formatting, 162
Undo button, Quick Access Toolbar, 77
undoing AutoCorrect changes, 74

Unhide Columns command, 40
unmatched records, 116–17
Update queries, 119
Use Control Wizards option, 132
user interface, 5–6

V

validation, data, 63
Validation Rule box, 63
Value Axis Gridlines button, 175
values
   adding with AutoCorrect, 76
   calculating, 113
   default, 61
   finding, 122–23
   largest, finding, 122
   reports, 134
   smallest, finding, 123
   updating, 119
vertical scroll bar, 14
vertical scroll box, 23
viewing tables, 22
views, object, 30
Views group, Home tab, 6
Vista, Windows, 14

W

Web files, saving objects as, 210–11
Web help, 18
Web pages, hyperlinks, 195
window, Access, 12
window control buttons, 12
Windows Vista, 14
Word, exporting data to, 214–15
Word tables, 10
Work Essentials site, 18
writing queries to tables, 118

X

XML data
   exporting, 208–09
   importing, 202–03
XOR operator, 112

Y–Z

yes/no data type, 52
zero-length strings, 60

About the Author

Curt Frye is a freelance writer and Microsoft Office Excel Most Valuable Professional from Portland, Oregon. He is the author of *Microsoft Office Excel 2007 Step By Step, Microsoft Office Excel 2007 Plain & Simple, Microsoft Office Access 2007 Plain & Simple,* and numerous articles for the Microsoft Office Work Essentials Web site.

What do you think of this book?

We want to hear from you!

Do you have a few minutes to participate in a brief online survey?

Microsoft is interested in hearing your feedback so we can continually improve our books and learning resources for you.

To participate in our survey, please visit:

www.microsoft.com/learning/booksurvey/

...and enter this book's ISBN-10 number (appears above barcode on back cover*). As a thank-you to survey participants in the United States and Canada, each month we'll randomly select five respondents to win one of five $100 gift certificates from a leading online merchant. At the conclusion of the survey, you can enter the drawing by providing your e-mail address, which will be used for prize notification only.

Thanks in advance for your input. Your opinion counts!

*Where to find the ISBN-10 on back cover

ISBN-13: 000-0-0000-00000-0
ISBN-10: 0-0000-00000-0

00000

0 000000 000000

Example only. Each book has unique ISBN.

www.microsoft.com/learning/booksurvey/